IT'S THE
LITTLE
THINGS

Gill & Macmillan
Hume Avenue, Park West, Dublin 12
www.gillmacmillanbooks.ie

978 07171 6365 6

Edited by Alison Walsh
Design and print origination by Fidelma Slattery
Printed and bound by CPI Group (UK) Ltd, CR0 4YY

This book is typeset in Perpetua and Saint Agnes.

The paper used in this book comes from the wood pulp
of managed forests. For every tree felled, at least one
tree is planted, thereby renewing natural resources.

A CIP catalogue record for this book is available from the
British Library.

It's the

Little
Things

Francis
Brennan's
Guide to
Life

GILL & MACMILLAN

CONTENTS

PLANES, TRAINS AND AUTOMOBILES · 101

THE WORLD OF WORK · 125

THE ANCIENT ART OF GROOMING: HOW TO LOOK YOUR BEST ON EVERY OCCASION · 149

In life, it's the little things that make us happy. It's the consideration shown by a child towards their parents, the care a host puts into creating a warm, cosy atmosphere, the sense of community created when neighbours look out for each other. And what these little things come down to can be summed up in one word: manners.

When I set out to write my 'Guide to Life', I didn't expect to write about manners—it sounds so old fashioned. I've never wanted to tell people how to behave. And, in this day and age, is there even any need? We're all modern now, with our texting and our smartphones and our casual suppers; maybe manners and etiquette belong to another time.

But once I thought about it, I realised that it all depends on what you think manners are. For me, they're about respect and making others happy and comfortable. It's my belief in life. As luck would have it, working at the Park Hotel Kenmare, I'm in a job where I'm able to do that; my business is making people happy. I keep the staff at the hotel happy, I make people happy and I'm a happy person myself.

'That's grand, Francis,' I hear you say, 'but we don't all work in the hospitality industry. Making people happy isn't *my* job, so what has it got to do with me?' 'Everything,' is my answer. You don't have to run a hotel to care about other people, or to know how to address a baronet, or even to know what cutlery to use at a formal dinner. Manners aren't about class or 'breeding', God help us. As far as I'm concerned, manners are about respect for others—respect and consideration. And there's no reason at all to think that we don't need respect for others in this day and age.

It's true that things are a lot more casual than they were when I was growing up. Sometimes I look at family and friends at the dinner table, wandering back and forth to play computer games and the like, and I want to throw my hands up in despair. That's not the way things were done in my day, but I know also that times change. Writing this book, I've come to understand that what really matters has remained the same: putting others first. As that great expert on manners Emily Post put it, 'Manners are a sensitive awareness of the feelings of others. If you have that awareness, you have good manners, no matter what fork you use.'

Emily Post was writing about manners at a time when a man was required to take off his hat when a woman entered a lift and to put it on again only 'in the corridor', and when all invitations had to be issued in the third person, preferably engraved. It seems so quaint nowadays, but what really struck me was how much of what she had to say was about simple consideration for other human beings—as relevant today as it was almost a hundred years ago. And yet, at the same time, things have changed: maybe it's no longer appropriate for a gentleman to stand when a lady comes into the room, or for him on no account to remove his shoes in company—we can relax a little on that score. But now, more than ever, we have to remember others. That's what I believe. It's what my mother taught me, and it's what I've learned from years of making other people happy. And I'd like to share some of that with you in this book.

It's all about the three circles of life, as I like to call it: home, community and the wider world. Manners begin at home, I think. It's where I was taught and where you're probably going to teach your children. If we don't teach our children the basics we'll raise a bunch of savages! So, in the early chapters of the book I'll look at the kind of things you learn at home. Yes, that includes table manners and whether or not you think elbows on the table matter a lot, or how to use a cheese knife. You'll still want to make sure your son or daughter knows not to talk while eating; you'll still want to teach them how to sit around a table and have a chat without needing to get up and consult Facebook every five minutes, and how to help themselves to the veg without stretching across your dinner plate. It's not about being Victorian: it's about consideration for others around the table.

This extends to your friends too. Your home is your castle, and you want your guests to feel that they're honoured invitees and that you're going to the trouble of looking nice and making a bit of an effort with dinner to show them how much you care. That doesn't mean that you have to serve twelve courses and snails for starters just to make them feel comfortable and welcome. And you might pick up some handy tips. Have you ever thought about how to make a good, hot cup of tea in a pot or how to whip up a batch of scones for a last-minute visitor? It's what I like to call that extra sprinkling of sparkle dust, making things that little bit more magical for your company and for you. I truly believe that that's what it's all about—the little things that make life run that bit more smoothly.

Then there are the manners we need when we're going outside the front door: the simple thank you to the man in the shop, the tip to your hairdresser (and, yes, you should tip: they don't get paid much), the cheery hello to your neighbour, even if you can't stand their barking dog or the way they leave the bins out in front of your gate. Good manners will make their day and yours. Maybe tipping your postman seems like a notion from another age, but, let me tell you, they will be a friend for life. Nowadays, community matters more than ever. Whether we live with Mother, Father and six kids or live alone, whether we're on the residents' committee in our little area or not, 'community' is about sharing the world we live in with others. Sometimes, in our virtual world, it's hard to remember that there's a real one out there, with real people, just like us.

In the real world, that third circle of life, we'll need to remember our manners in the office, whether it's a van, a garden shed or an open-plan space. We'll need to think of others when we're eating out and also when travelling, but that doesn't always mean doing so at our own expense. As Theodore Roosevelt said, politeness is 'a sign of dignity, not subservience.' For example, I travel a lot on aeroplanes, and, to be honest, I don't talk to anybody on a flight—absolutely no way—because if you talk to someone on a five-hour flight you have to talk all the way. And if I do talk I enjoy it, but then I'm exhausted afterwards, because I'm always 'on stage'. A plane, for me, is an opportunity to read a book or listen to music, to be 'dilly-dreamy', as my mother used to say. I say, 'Good morning,' and not another word. There's nothing wrong with that: having good manners doesn't mean having to be a doormat or to exhaust yourself in the service of others.

What I'd also like to do in this book is help you glide through those potentially awkward social occasions—weddings, funerals, christenings—the kind of formal occasions that can make you into a nervous wreck if you don't know how to handle them. I've attended plenty of formal occasions in my lifetime, and, while protocol is important, the key is to relax and to know that you're a valued guest. In our casual world, fine dining can often induce a fit of the heebie-jeebies. I aim to take the mystery out of that, so that you can relax and enjoy the magnificent food and the lovely surroundings. I'll also look at how we present ourselves, as how we look can often influence how we feel.

For me, manners aren't a rigid set of rules. They're not there to trip you up or to embarrass you, or to put you in some kind of a straitjacket; they're not there to interfere with you living your life. They're more a set of principles to live by: caring, consideration, community—the three Cs, I like to call them! And I hope that this little book will give you a fourth C—confidence—to go out there and show the world what a great person you are.

Manners
begin
at
home

'It's all in the house.'
—Bill Cosby, 2004

I KNOW this will probably make me sound a bit old-fashioned, but I firmly believe that manners begin at home. As a colleague of mine said when I told him I was writing a book on etiquette, 'Oh, that's all the stuff your mother taught you.' Brilliant, isn't it? And it's true: along with teaching you to tie your shoelaces, comb your hair and brush your teeth properly, mothers—and fathers, these days—also teach children those essential skills that will take them through life.

That's what manners are, I think: not fussy instructions about how to fold napkins and that kind of thing, but respect, and that works both ways. In my house my mother had respect for us, and we had respect for her. I'm not a parent, but I understand the valuable lessons my mother taught me. To my parents, manners weren't about being strict or laying down the law, but about being a child's guide in life. That's the golden rule, as far as I'm concerned: if you show them how it's done—being polite to others around you—your children will follow.

My parents expected things of us. My father, a grocer, expected us all to help out on Saturdays and during the summer holidays. He had a van for making deliveries to the estates that were being built around Dublin in the 1960s, and we helped him load it with supplies. At home we cut the grass as soon as we were old enough, and we helped out around the house. We were also expected to be polite to the neighbours and to adults in general. I suppose that many people were in awe of the parish priest or the doctor in those days, but to my parents it was all about respect.

Nowadays we're all about giving our children confidence: telling them how well they're doing and how great they are and to express themselves. That's wonderful, of course, but we also need to teach them how to get along with others. That's what manners are all about. If little Fergus lets out a big scream every time he wants our attention, he'll certainly make himself heard, but he won't learn that he can just say, 'Excuse me.' And when he's twenty-five he can't scream in a business meeting! The same goes for other kinds of behaviour—the kind of thing we might think is 'cute', like monopolising the conversation with a long story about school, or dancing up and down to get our attention. At home we might turn a blind eye to it, but what happens when you're in the supermarket or trying to talk to a friend?

DECIDING ON THE BASICS

Every family will have its own standards when it comes to manners. Some families might insist that children wait until everyone has finished eating before getting up from the table; others might not care about that kind of thing at all. Some people are quite happy to leave the television on while they eat; others insist on switching it off. Establish what the ground rules are in your house by deciding what you think is important, whether it's eating peas with a fork or not interrupting others at the table. It doesn't have to be rocket science, just a few simple rules, because if you get the basics right the rest will follow. And keep it positive—no *don'ts*, just *dos*:

$\mathcal{D}o$:

· Listen to others ·
· Wait for your turn to speak ·

· Tidy your plate into the dishwasher
when you've finished eating ·
· Wait at the table after you've eaten ·
· Close your mouth when you're eating ·
· Try to eat as quietly as you can, without crunching,
slurping or burping, for that matter! ·
· Use your knife and fork ·
· Offer to help Mammy and Daddy clear up afterwards ·
· Say 'Excuse me' when you want Mammy
or Daddy's attention ·
· Say 'Please' and 'Thank you' ·

Not hard, and not a *don't* in sight! And there are also simple ways to ensure that your children absorb more easily the lessons you have to teach them. I'm a strong believer in families eating together, because it's a great training ground for manners. My father would come home for lunch every day, and because lunch was the main meal in those days, my brother and I would even come home from school, getting the bus all the way from Westland Row home to Balally and then back again—a round trip of about eight miles. If the bus was late we'd be late for school. I always remember, if it was apple and custard for dessert, my mother would have it on the back step to cool—that's the truth—because you had to eat it so quickly!

Of course, these days you can't be getting your son or daughter home from school for lunch every day, but you can try to make eating as a family a regular occurrence. Who was it who said, 'The family that eats together stays together'? When a family is eating together they're talking together, chatting about the day and what's been happening. You might find out that your son or daughter really likes sport, or hates it, had a disagreement with a teacher or got an A in a science test, and while you're having your lovely conversation you can be teaching them those essential life skills: wait your turn to speak, close your mouth when you're eating, say 'Excuse me' when you want to get other people's attention. Eating together also really helps if your children are fussy eaters: seeing you happily tucking into salmon will make them think it's delicious!

The other great thing about teaching manners is that your children will behave as you'd like them to when you're in company. I still remember a visit from my mother's old land-lady, who had the great name of Mrs Lemon. My mother had stayed with her in digs and wanted to show her new home off to her. I was five, and my brother Damien was six. Mum had decided to serve a whole chicken, which was a real luxury in those days, and before Mrs Lemon arrived she warned us, 'Now, be on your best behaviour, and don't ask for more.' In my home we called it 'FHB'—family hold back! When dinner was finished, Mum was clearing the plates, and Damien piped up, 'Pass the plate, Mrs Lemon. It has bones on it, and Mammy always uses the bones to make soup.' Needless to say, Mammy was mortified.

On the subject of eating in public, I'm always amazed to see parents not taking responsibility for their children's be-haviour in a restaurant or café. They say, 'That's nothing to do with me.' Well, it is, but the good news is that if you've put the groundwork in at home, your outings should run that bit more smoothly. But don't be afraid to be assertive. One night in America I was out at a restaurant, and there was a family with small children beside me. They were immediately given colouring books and then brown bread and slices of banana, without their parents having to ask. I thought it was a brilliant idea, as the kids were happy and didn't get hungry or tired. If your local restaurant doesn't do this, why not ask? It's common sense for restaurateurs not to want a screaming child on their hands, so they should be only too happy to help.

SHARING SPACE

When we all live in the same house, it makes sense that we should share all the household tasks. I get on great with my friend's teenager, but he has never in his life opened or closed the dishwasher. He drops everything in the bathroom, and when his mother returns from a day or two away she can't get into the laundry room, because it's full of his discarded clothes. It's not hard to see that when he goes to live on his own he won't know that he has to pick up his own clothes and wash his own dishes. And it's not his fault. Sharing household tasks teaches kids to respect life later on, and it makes life run much more smoothly right now, when all of us are so busy.

You can start with age-appropriate jobs, such as tidying plates and glasses into the dishwasher or putting the salt and pepper back into the cupboard. Small children want to please Mammy or Daddy, so we can use this to our advantage. When I was growing up we all had small jobs: I used to cut the grass and do the hedge and garden from the age of twelve or thirteen, and my sisters used to vacuum the house on Saturdays. Of course, your five-year-old won't quite be up to the job of cutting the grass, but there are lots of small jobs they can help with: tidying their room, making their bed, tidying up their books and Lego, and, later on, running the vacuum-cleaner around the house or helping Dad put the bins out. Some of these little jobs might involve persuasion on your part, but it's worth it, because you're teaching them skills for life.

For many parents, getting their kids to help out around the house is also about teaching them to take responsibility for themselves, which is why mums and dads get so annoyed when the jobs aren't done. They despair, because they think their messy teenagers will never take responsibility for the dirty bedrooms, the damp towels left on the bed, and the piles of dirty plates and cereal bowls in the sink for 'somebody' to wash up. In that case, it's time for the rota! Setting aside specific jobs for each family member to do every week might well be the answer if you're exhausted nagging. It can help to set aside a couple of hours—on a Saturday morning, say—when everyone does their chores at the same time. This has the advantage of sparing you from having to nag more than one child at a time. I have friends who don't part with pocket money until all the children's chores are finished, which is one approach. Others make sure that their children take responsibility for any pets: cleaning out rabbit hutches and taking Fido for a walk are great ways for children to learn to be responsible.

I would advise parents not to get too excited about standards, however, at least for smaller children. Your six-year-old isn't going to be able to vacuum the living room as well as you can: instead, reward them for effort, which really works, I'm told. Yes, it probably is easier and quicker to do things yourself, but children get great satisfaction out of doing little jobs as best they can and earning Mum's or Dad's praise.

When your children are teenagers it will be time to work on their practical skills, teaching them basic recipes and making sure they know how to do their laundry, use the iron and clean the bathroom properly. They're in the departure lounge for adult life, after all, and soon they'll have to manage without you. You don't want them being the flatmate from hell either!

THE SMALLEST ROOM IN THE HOUSE

I spend a lot of time in America on business, and nobody there knows about a thing called the 'immersion': hot water is always there, and people can have showers whenever they like. Not so in Ireland. Des Bishop has a very funny skit on the immersion—'You mean I have to heat the water myself?'—imagining himself on a bicycle pedalling to get the shower to work!

It's true that in this country resources are more expensive, so we have to establish some ground rules about sharing them.

- If you want to use the shower, ask. If it's not an electric shower, it may well be that someone else has turned on the immersion to have a shower before an important interview or to go out for the night, and they won't be happy if you've used up all the water.

- Try not to spend so long in the shower that all the hot water runs out. There's nothing more unpleasant than having to rinse out hair in cold water.

- Switch off the immersion afterwards. A kitchen timer—set to five minutes, say—can be a great help in reminding people to get out of the shower.

- Clean up after yourself following your shower. Put your damp towels away and pick your clothes up off the floor.

- Rinse the bath out. Nobody really wants your grubby footprints, and worse, in the bath!

- Always flush the toilet and put the seat down. And if you've used up the last of the toilet roll put another one in the holder. The toilet roll should always be pulled from the front, with the sheets coming over the top. A nice touch is to point pleat the first sheet on the roll into a triangle.

- Don't use up someone else's expensive shower gel. But if you do, own up—don't just put the empty bottle in the bin!

When it comes to other shared spaces, it's important to remember that they are *shared*, and that you might have to make more of an effort to keep them tidy and not spread stuff all over the place. (This applies to adults as well as children, by the way.) My mother had a rule about never eating in the living room, but if this doesn't bother you remind everyone to tidy up after themselves and not leave smelly trainers under the sofa and that kind of thing. Decide where your boundaries lie and observe them. If you don't want the dog on the sofa, put its basket on the floor with something nice in it to encourage it to use it. If you want your son or daughter to tidy up their toys, let them know that the television will be switched on only when the toys are tidied away. My friends tell me that consistency is the best policy here!

PRIVACY

I think it works both ways in a shared home, whether you're sharing a student flat or living with your family. If your teenage son or daughter is in their room, always knock before you go in: it's their private space. In a family home you shouldn't need locks on the doors, because everybody should respect each other's privacy. The same goes for other people's possessions: if your son or daughter has a diary I think it's best to resist the urge to snoop, unless they're in some kind of danger. If you'd rather your children didn't rummage through your old love letters or peek at that mortgage application, tuck them away somewhere private. And you can respectfully ask them not to rummage.

Of course, in many family homes and shared flats the fridge can become a bit of a battleground. If you don't want to get to the stage of leaving rude notes on your cheese or waving an empty carton of milk angrily at your teenage child, set some ground rules: whoever empties the carton has to go and get more; keep your stuff in a Tupperware box or allocate shelving on which to keep your food; and agree that all unused food will be thrown out on a Friday, to avoid the spectacle of three-week-old food with mould on it.

The eggs and the fire brigade

This last comment—and the one before it, about being just too nosy for your own good—reminds me of the story of the eggs and the fire brigade. I used to work in Jury's Hotel, as the night manager of the Coffee Dock. You had to be on your toes, because there was always a huge queue, it being one of the few late-night places in the city. I used to work with the Mothers of Ireland, grand country girls who'd worked there for years because the money and tips were good; but sometimes they'd get up to mischief. In the kitchen was a double door to the deep freeze, on top of which was a brown box. It had been there for about five months, but I'd done nothing about it apart from, on the odd occasion, wonder what was in it.

On one particular night I was working away at the door, showing people to their table, when I heard a huge scream, followed shortly after by an unearthly smell. 'What on earth is that?' I thought, as the customers all jumped up and ran out, fearing that it might be some kind of gas leak. I charged into the kitchen, and here were two of the Mothers of Ireland, looking terrified and covered in a sticky, translucent substance.

In a fit of nosiness, one had hooshed the other up to examine the contents of the box and had pulled it over, break-ing the seal in the process. It turned out that it had contained liquid egg white—often used in the restaurant business—but it had long gone off, and now they were covered in it from head to toe. We had to evacuate the restaurant and get the fire brigade to clear the smell of sulphur. 'Leave well enough alone' is the moral of the story!

ACROSS THE GENERATIONS

It's not uncommon nowadays, with so many people living into their eighties and even nineties, and with the younger generation finding it harder to afford their own homes, to have more than one generation living under your roof. I think consideration becomes even more important if you're one big multi-generational family. Perhaps Granny or

Granddad has an illness and needs to take medicine or can't drive any more. The older members of the household will also need their own space, including their own bathroom, in all likelihood. They will probably also have a different routine and different interests from their teenage grandchildren. And while many grandparents are happy to help out with babysitting, they won't like to be taken for granted or feel that they provide babysitting on tap, so it's good to be aware of this. On the other hand, many people don't like to have the benefit of their parents' 'old-fashioned' views, so, Granny and Granddad: be restrained and try not to interfere in the way your son or daughter does things.

But so many people talk about the great benefits of living with other generations. For children, there's always someone to talk to and share stories with—and to let off steam with, if Mum or Dad is being unreasonable—and they love hearing Granny's and Granddad's stories of the old days. Also, many grandparents find that living with the younger generation gives them a real boost and helps them to look at the world in a new way.

BEING THE PERFECT HOST

If we've got the basics right, and the house isn't some kind of war zone, we should be able to invite people in for a meal or a cup of tea and to show off our beautifully behaved children!

But because we're so busy nowadays and so pressed for time, inviting guests into our home—whether for ten minutes or a weekend—can seem a bit daunting. But with a few basics, and that all-important bit of planning, you'll sail smoothly through the whole thing.

First of all, those basics. Make sure your house is warm. Now, this may seem fairly obvious, but with our damp climate it's not always a given. We all know how unpleasant it can be to go into a friend's freezing-cold house with that horrible draught at the back of our neck. It doesn't exactly encourage us to stay! So, a warm welcome, with heat, is very important.

If you're making tea or coffee, make it fresh: try not to stew the tea or offer your guest something reheated. I'm a great believer in a proper, hot cup of tea, served from a teapot, because I think it looks so much nicer than a tea bag dunked up and down in a mug of hot water for a few minutes.

I came across an essay by George Orwell in the *Evening Standard* on the very subject; clearly he was a tea man. Among his instructions was to always use Indian or 'Ceylonese' (Sri Lankan) tea. Chinese tea has its virtues, he said, but 'one does not feel wiser, braver or more optimistic after drinking it.' Having chosen the right tea, you were then to make sure that the teapot was warmed—fair enough—and that the tea was nice and strong, which he acknowledged might be difficult, because it was 1946 and tea rationing was still in place. He also recommended something that reminded me of what my mother used to say: 'Take the teapot to the kettle and not the other way around.' This was to ensure that the water was actually boiling when it was poured over the tea.

HERE'S HOW
I MAKE IT

1.

Put the kettle on to boil.

2.

When it has almost boiled, splash some of the hot water into the teapot and swish it around to warm the pot. You can use a china pot or a stainless-steel one. I prefer china, because it looks so nice and I think the flavour's better.

3.

Empty the pot, then pop in your tea leaves or bags. I don't have a preference, as I think there are some very nice tea bags around at the moment and some lovely flavours, but some people insist on real tea leaves. If you're using leaves, a teaspoon of leaves for each person plus one for the pot is the usual rule of thumb.

4.

Make sure the water is boiling properly; have your teapot beside the kettle and pour the boiling water over the leaves or bags. This is the most important step. If you haven't got a kettle, make sure the water is boiling furiously in the saucepan. (That's 100°C, for those of you who remember your science lessons.)

5.

Leave the tea to draw. Five minutes will be just perfect. Anything shorter and you'll have 'gnat's pee', as my granny used to call it. A friend of mine says that if you can stand a spoon up in it, it's perfect, but I don't like it quite that strong. If you're using a china pot use a tea cosy, because you don't want the tea to go cold.

6.

Some people like to warm the cups as well, but this shouldn't be necessary if the tea is nice and hot. I always pour the tea first and then add the milk, because that way you can judge how much milk the tea needs. Enjoy!

The silver teapot

While I'm on the subject of tea, my favourite tea story is one from my mother. She lived in digs in Ranelagh in 1949, on Beechwood Avenue, with a very strict landlady who kept an eye on the young ladies of the house. Of course, no sooner had the landlady gone away for the weekend to Westport than my mother and the woman's daughter, who were great friends, decided to have a party. Four hundred people turned up, and it was one of *those* parties—the kind everyone remembers.

But then, the next morning, my mother noticed that the landlady's china cabinet was open, and her prized silver teapot, which stood on three silver legs, seemed to be missing. At first Mum thought it had been stolen, but then she noticed, to her horror, that someone had taken it out and left it on the gas stove, with the result that one of the legs had melted. The teapot was over at an angle, like a drunken sailor. My mother was in an awful panic: if she lost her place in the digs she'd be mortified, and, as she'd got a prized job in the civil service, she knew she'd never live it down if she was sent home to Sligo in disgrace.

That morning she bumped into a friend who'd been at the party. 'Oh, Maura, that was the best party ever,' he said.

'I never want to talk about it again,' Mum said. 'Someone burned the leg off the silver teapot!'

'Oh, I might be able to do something,' her friend said cheerfully. 'I know a fellow who can do a job on that for you.'

Mum was delighted. 'Make sure you have it back after lunch, because the landlady's coming back on the four o'clock train,' she warned him.

As good as his word, he returned with the teapot and put it down on the table, where it sat nicely, and they all admired it. It took them a while to notice that he'd simply chopped the other two legs off the pot! They put it back in the china cabinet, and the landlady never noticed.

✳

A LITTLE EXTRA...

While we might not all have time to whip up a freshly baked batch of scones, or sandwiches with the crusts cut off, to accompany our pot of tea, you can put a few biscuits on a plate or cut a few slices of shop-bought cake—anything to look as if you value your guest. I always have a packet of nice biscuits hidden away for that possibility. If you have a bit of soda bread, there's nothing nicer than a slick of butter and a spoon of jam on it. Use a separate spoon for the sugar bowl and pour milk into a milk jug, rather than putting a plastic carton on the table. Here's a nice recipe from the Park Hotel Kenmare for a quick scone mix, if you have time.

Park Hotel Kenmare scones (makes twelve)

280 g plain flour	150 ml buttermilk
¼ tsp baking powder	Seeds of ¼ of a vanilla pod,
½ tsp salt	scraped out
130 g unsalted butter	60 g sultanas
70 g sugar	Zest of one orange
1 large egg	

- Combine flour, baking powder and salt, and sift into a large mixing bowl.
- Cut in butter with a pastry blender or rub it in using your fingers until mixture resembles coarse crumbs.
- Add sugar and mix well.
- Add egg, milk and vanilla pod seeds, and mix well.
- Add sultanas and orange zest and blend thoroughly.
- Turn out onto a lightly floured surface and roll to a half-inch thickness.
- Cut into rounds using a 2½ inch / 5 cm biscuit-cutter and place on an ungreased baking sheet.
- Bake at 325°F / Gas mark 3 / 170°C for 14 to 17 minutes or until bottoms are firm. Remove from oven and place scones on a wire rack to cool.
- *Serve with butter, freshly whipped or clotted cream and fresh raspberries or jam.*

✳

HAVING SOMEONE TO STAY

I think there's no greater challenge to a friendship than having someone to stay in your home; but it can often be the sign of a good friendship that the two of you can see each other at such close quarters and still remain pals. But, as in anything else in life, a few simple rules for the host and the guest will really help the visit to run smoothly and keep your friendship intact.

First of all, it's much better to say no to their visit if it doesn't suit you than to seethe with resentment for their entire stay. They may well have come from Australia for a weekend, but if you're just about to go on holiday, or your house is being done up, there's no harm at all in saying no or in offering to put them up in a local B&B. However, if you're only too delighted to be having them, the key is to welcome them into your home, but not let them run all over it. It's your home and they need to fit in with your way of doing things, not the other way round. Still, it's really nice to make an effort for your guests to show them how welcome they are. Here are a few basics:

- You may not have a spare bedroom, only a sofa, but you can still make it comfortable for your guests. A set of fresh bed linen (pillowcase openings should always face away from the entrance to the room) and clean towels will be perfect, perhaps with a few magazines to give things that homely feel. You can also give them a reading-lamp and some water.

- Show them where everything is when they arrive and where they can help themselves to tea, coffee, milk, bread, toilet roll, the TV remote, etc. On the other hand, if you don't want them helping themselves to your precious Kenyan blend or your posh muesli, best to just discreetly put these items away.

- You might like to let your guests know what your busy times are as a family so that there won't be any clashes about breakfast or bathroom times.

- The bathroom can be a tricky area for Irish hosts. We don't have a number of en-suites, unlike our American cousins, so you might have to explain the ground rules here, such as when it's best to use the shower and if the toilet needs to be flushed twice. And put the toilet seat down! You might also like to keep a spare toothbrush handy. (We had a young man who used to come and stay with us and who never brought his own toothbrush. We used to have to hide our toothbrushes discreetly to let him know that he'd have to buy his own! Maybe he had only one toothbrush at home...)

- Leave things out on the kitchen table for the guests if they will be getting up and out before you. If they will be needing transport give them directions to the bus stop or taxi rank. You don't need to drive them to the airport, unless you really have the time or really want to—airport bus services are so good nowadays. You might also like to pick up some tourist leaflets and leave them out for your guests.

• Remember that if you have guests you're not alone any more, so if you like to wander around the house naked, now is not the time! On the other hand, if you always do Pilates on a Wednesday, it's perfectly fine to say that and to ask your guests to entertain themselves for an hour.

BEING A DREAM GUEST

As a guest, you want your host to be only too happy to invite you back, so it's important to be a good guest. The golden rule is never to stay longer than three days: any longer and you'll wear your hosts out and have them secretly wondering when you might be going home. Here are a few tips to leave your hosts wanting more:

• Bring a little gift with you. It doesn't have to be anything too elaborate, just something small. I think it's nice to send something in advance so that your host is looking forward to seeing you. They'll love a bunch of flowers sent three or four days before your visit. Or, when you're there, take them out for dinner: it can be a really nice thank you for a family who might not go out that often.

• If there's a little contretemps between Mr and Mrs when you're visiting, it's time to make yourself scarce. Say nothing; just go to bed early and read your book.

• Don't help yourself to the last of the bread, breakfast cereal or coffee. If you do, replace it. You might have noticed a local corner shop on your way where you can pick up a loaf of bread.

- Offer to help with the washing-up or bedtime routines if your host has young children. Some hosts are delighted to have a night off from bedtime stories, but if they prefer to do things themselves don't get in the way.

- You'll have to fit in with the family's style of eating and their mealtimes. Of course, if you're a vegetarian, for example, don't announce it at the dinner table: if you have special dietary needs it's really best to let your hosts know in advance. If you simply dislike spaghetti bolognese, don't say, 'No, thanks, I can't stand it.' Politely say that you had a big lunch earlier and that a sandwich will do you.

- Don't wander around the house or in and out of bedrooms unless your host invites you to do so. This is their private space, and you need to respect that.

- Keep your bedroom or sofa corner tidy—no luggage or underwear strewn around!

- Say thank you. A little something left on the kitchen table, a bottle left in the fridge or a bunch of flowers on departure will be much appreciated.

If you've mastered the art of hosting and have graduated by having a guest, you're now ready to move on to dinner parties, which I cover in the next chapter. But the most important thing when hosting is to enjoy it. As Aeschylus said, 'What is there more kindly than the feeling between host and guest?'

Guess who's coming to dinner?

'After a good dinner one can forgive anybody, even one's own relations.'
—*Oscar Wilde*, A Woman of No Importance

The ostrich

I have a little cottage at the end of my garden in Kenmare, and every year I invite old friends to stay—about eight lads I used to go to school with, some of whom became priests. They take it in turns to cook something really special for their fellow guests. One year it was the turn of my friend Martin, who is a Marist in Paris. He really wanted to push the boat out, so he rang me up and asked me if I could get ostrich. (This was twenty years ago, when ostrich was unheard of.) I rang my brother Damien, who was working for Tourism Ireland, and he said Neven Maguire might be the man, because he was very much on the cutting edge of food.

Sure enough, Neven said he could get it, but it only came as frozen. True to his word, he got the ostrich and it was sent to me by way of Damien in Sligo. I was surprised when it arrived down to Kenmare in a shoebox; all you got was the ostrich breasts, though they were huge—much bigger than turkey.

Martin came in to talk to my chef, Brian Cleere, about how to cook the ostrich. Brian had worked in Australia for many years and had loads of experience with ostrich and alligator and that kind of thing. They happily discussed the ostrich, marinades and cooking times, and then Martin left, happy with his new-found knowledge and confident about producing a show-stopper.

They'd been overheard by a young man, a commis chef at the time, who asked Brian, 'What were you talking about there?'

'Oh, that man wanted to know how to cook ostrich and I was telling him, because I've cooked it loads of times,' replied Brian.

'Oh, right,' said the young man, a puzzled look on his face. 'Ostrich…' he murmured. 'How would you get an ostrich in the oven?' The poor man visualised Martin trying to squeeze an entire ostrich into the oven, head, legs and all. The moral of the story, when it comes to dinner parties, is to keep things simple!

DINNER PARTIES

I'm a great giver of dinner parties: I love having friends around, and it's a great way to entertain. But, for so many of us, the very idea of a dinner party makes us quake with anxiety. I think the problem can be that we don't plan enough, and then we find ourselves racing around the place with a big red face, throwing things in and out of the oven, instead of sitting down with our guests and a nice glass of something in the living room. Planning is the key for any kind of party but particularly for dinner parties.

The other thing to bear in mind before you get started is who you want to invite. Have a good think about this, because not all your friends will gel: sometimes the only thing they have in common is you, or if they do have a common interest, like hillwalking or the book club, they might struggle to chat outside that structure. If it's a work dinner party they might not even know you, in which case it's even more of a challenge. Maybe the novelist Marian Keyes was right when she said, 'I'd rather dig a ditch than go to a dinner party with people I don't know.' This can apply to either work dinners or those with 'friends'. Some people really enjoy getting different groups together and are happy to mix all kinds of people, because they think it might be interesting. If this is the case for you, try to embrace it and have a little fun with it if you can. The other people at the party are likely to be as nervous as you are about talking to strangers—you're all in the same boat!

When it comes to work dinners, they can be awkward affairs, because the intimate setting doesn't seem to square with what is essentially a business meeting. Try to remember that it's a way of getting to know your client or customer better, which is all to your advantage. Some people aren't bothered by work dinners—maybe they figure that if it's a disaster they won't have to see their business contacts again!—but others find them a complete ordeal. I think the most important thing to remember is that it *is* work and that you're not really expected to let your hair down. Drinking wine is acceptable with the meal, but you won't make a good impression on your boss if you drink too much.

Also, if it's a business dinner, consider whether you're going to 'seal the deal' at the dinner itself or whether the main business will be conducted afterwards, as this will dictate the course of the conversation. You won't need to launch into your knowledge of share prices over the soup, so you can relax a little. And there's no reason at all not to have a handy list of conversational openers in your pocket or handbag, or not to have done your homework on your guests and their interests beforehand. It's only natural that when we're conversing with strangers we run out of steam sometimes, and these prompts might well help to restart a stalled conversation.

MUST-HAVE INVITATIONS

Once you've decided who you're going to invite, it's time to invite them. The days of the hand-engraved invitation have gone, but I think things have gone a bit too far in the other direction, and the result is that people can feel they aren't that valued as guests. The group text message or e-mail just doesn't feel that special to me. Also, texts aren't good with subtlety or humour, and you can accidentally give the wrong impression. I always make a phone call. It's as personal as you can be nowadays to phone somebody and ask if they're free on Saturday and to say you'd love to see them. This also has the benefit of getting people to commit themselves to the event in good time.

If, like me, you invite a gang of friends over for dinner to celebrate your birthday, I'd suggest that you invite no more than eight people. At the hotel, when we take wedding bookings the bride-to-be often says, 'Oh, you only have tables for eight. I prefer ten.' If you've ten people at a table the conversation doesn't flow; but if you've eight, every single person talks to every other person. My brother John does things this way at our wedding venue in Dromquinna Manor and he gets great reviews for his weddings, so I think you'll get great reviews for your dinner parties too.

If you invite someone but they're not sure they can make it, ask them if they can let you know by a certain time. That way you'll have time to find a substitute, if one is needed. Don't worry if your friend then decides they can make it after all: one dinner party with nine people instead of eight isn't a disaster. In fact, all your invitees should let you know in good time whether they can make it or not, so that you can plan your menu—no later than forty-eight hours before the event is my rule of thumb.

If your friend wants to invite their new partner you don't have to say yes: you can nicely say that of course you'd love to meet them sometime, but you'll have a full house on Friday. You can then suggest another time to meet. But if your friend will have a long-expected visitor from, say, the United States with them, try to be accommodating.

If you're invited to a dinner party try not to cancel at the last minute, unless of course there's an emergency. If you have two invitations for the same night the golden rule is accept one of them—or neither—but don't accept and then cancel if you get a better offer. These things have a way of backfiring on you, and you might find that you won't be very popular!

If you're a vegetarian or a vegan, or have other dietary needs, it's best to let your host know in advance. I'm sure they'd prefer this, and the fussing they might need to do to accommodate you, to finding out only when they've put the roast lamb in front of you!

THE MENU

If you're the host and have issued your invitations, it's time to plan the menu. What kind of menu you use will depend very much on what kind of dinner you're having—a Thursday-night bowl of pasta with a few close pals, a sit-down three-course meal for eight or a brunch for neighbours and family? No matter how informal the occasion, the key is to plan your menus and avoid doing everything on the night. I always do things I can prepare in advance, like a terrine or smoked salmon. Add a bit of salad and, hey presto! You have a lovely starter.

Barbecues are also a great, easy dinner: you can still be a bit formal in the sitting room, but you can cook your rib-eye steaks in the back garden. It's a very easy way of getting your main course done, because you prepare all your salads ahead of time. Also, a Sunday brunch or garden barbecue is a great way of entertaining guests who you owe a turn to, so to speak, but who you might not really want to become your closest buddies. It can also be a great way of entertaining more than one generation: the kids can run around the garden while you look after Granny inside.

Generally speaking, simple and easy really is best with a dinner party. I was with friends in Dallas before St Patrick's Day one year, and one of them asked my advice on what to prepare for an Irish dinner party. I suggested smoked salmon and brown soda bread, because they can both be bought in the shop, and soda bread is the easiest thing in the world to make. This could be followed by a big pot of Irish stew, because it's delicious if you do it properly, and it can be prepared the day before. (In fact, it gets nicer if it's made that way.) Also, my friend has a lovely Waterford Crystal bowl, so I suggested she use it to make a traditional trifle, with the layers of custard, jelly and cream, which was a real novelty for her. She had a fantastic dinner party, and it was all done in advance.

If you want to prepare beforehand, think about each course and what you could do for it. Some dinner-party experts swear by the formula of a cold starter and dessert and a hot main course as the simplest way of ensuring success. Others like to plan around a theme, such as an Indian night, and group all their dishes around that. Here are a few ideas to get you started.

STARTERS
❦

A simple *vegetable soup* is lovely on a winter's night—something like curried parsnip (lovely parsnip and onion softened, to which is added a teaspoon of old-fashioned curry powder and then a litre or so of stock) or perhaps sweet potato, if you'd like something exotic. A few slices of fried chorizo—a spicy Spanish sausage available in most supermarkets—will spice a bland soup up, or you could try something like broccoli and Stilton soup, which has a real kick. A chilled soup like gazpacho can be lovely during summertime. You can even try a 'white gazpacho', made with almonds and bread, which tastes delicious. Soup is very easy to prepare and leave in the fridge or on the stove.

We probably all remember the *chicken liver pâté* of the 1970s, and it's still delicious. Here's a recipe for that classic, which came from a friend of mine. It was shared with all her lady friends, so no-one can claim the original! It's not a low-fat recipe, but you'll be eating very small quantities.

✳

Chicken liver pâté

1 lb / 450 g chicken livers	1 small onion, chopped
½ lb / 220 g butter	2 tbsp mayonnaise
¼ lb / 110 g pancetta or	1 tbsp cream
chopped streaky bacon	2 tbsp brandy (optional)
Pinch of nutmeg	

- Trim any fat off the chicken livers and pop them into a pot along with the chopped onion, butter and pancetta (or streaky bacon) and a pinch of nutmeg.
- Bring the whole thing to a gentle sizzle for about twenty minutes, until the livers have lost their pinkness and are cooked through.
- Take the mixture out and put it in a blender—in batches if necessary—and blend it until smooth. You can freeze the mixture now, if using it later, or you can add the mayonnaise and cream and mix well. Now add the brandy, if using it, and give it another little stir.
- Put it into a suitable dish and leave it to set in the fridge for a couple of hours.
- Serve with Melba toast (very thinly sliced crustless white bread, toasted) or with toasted ciabatta loaf or crackers.

There are a number of alternatives to the richness of this recipe, all of which are easy to make and to serve with tiny slices of crisp toast. A smoked salmon pâté, made with cream cheese and dill, is particularly delicious, as is a smoked mackerel pâté—it couldn't be easier, and smoked fish is available in all supermarkets nowadays. There are also a number of tasty vegetarian pâtés, such as mushroom pâté or hummus, which you can make yourself from a combination of tinned chickpeas, garlic, olive oil and tahini paste, which is a sesame paste (or smooth peanut butter, if you're stuck) and a squeeze of lemon juice. There's also a delicious white-bean hummus, which tastes lovely and creamy. If you're really stuck for time your local deli will be able to serve you some nice pork terrine, which you can claim as your own!

✳

Antipasti are served cold. Salami with olives and nice bread and olive oil—that's antipasti! It means 'before the meal', a little plate of cold eats that Italians nibble on before their meal. Many supermarkets now sell prosciutto ham and Serrano ham, both of which are delicious, as well as salami, and you can then add olives, some nice bread and olive oil. You can also add sun-dried tomatoes or artichoke hearts, which are commonly available in jars in the supermarket.

You could make a *simple salad* of something like pear, crumbled blue cheese and toasted walnuts with rocket, which you can put together at the last minute. (It's fine to buy bagged salad leaves if you're in a hurry.) A Greek salad is also lovely and quick to do, with sliced red onions, tomatoes, cucumber, green peppers, black olives and cubed feta. And if you've been put off coleslaw by the horrible supermarket versions, remember that shredded cabbage and carrot with raisins, coated in a nice, mustardy mayonnaise, makes a lovely home-made accompaniment to cold meat.

MAIN COURSE

I'm a great fan of day-ahead dishes that can simply be reheated on the night. But remember, if you put anything in the freezer allow plenty of time for it to defrost.

Lasagne can be made the day before and reheated in the oven for twenty minutes. You can also do all kinds of variations, such as a roasted vegetable lasagne or one with salmon, if you prefer. A friend of mine recently made one with fennel and pumpkin, which was delicious.

A nice, fragrant *curry* can be an easy main course, but first check that you've no-one who doesn't like spicy food, in which case you can make a mild one. A chicken korma is a nice creamy version that should please everyone.

Any kind of *stew or casserole* is good for a dinner party, and you can also be adventurous with it: there's venison stew or lovely big artisan sausages with gravy, or even pork belly. A lovely Provençal fish stew is delicious, and if you've vegetarians you don't have to do the usual bean stew (!); try a Moroccan-style chickpea stew with lovely spices, which you can serve with couscous.

DESERT

I generally like to serve a cold dessert, because I think it's so much easier. If it's wintertime I just cook a nice hot dinner and then I don't have to worry about warm dessert. I like a baked cheesecake, which I make the day before and leave to chill—it won't spoil at room temperature, because it's cooked. I also think you can't go wrong with Eton mess (a mix of broken meringue, whipped cream and fruit) or a lovely home-made apple tart.

If pastry is too intimidating you can easily buy it chilled or frozen in the supermarket. Or make it a crumble—everyone loves a crumble, and you can use seasonal fruit. There can be nothing more delicious in life than apple-and-blackberry crumble! I also discovered a lovely roasted fruit dessert a few years ago: you roast fruit such as peaches and plums—any fruit with a stone in it, basically—in the oven with brown sugar and vanilla for about twenty minutes. You can serve this with Greek yoghurt.

Alternatively, there's no shame in buying something delicious for dessert, such as a lemon tart or a chocolate-mousse cake, if you've a good local deli or bakery nearby. Everyone understands that people are busy nowadays.

The French beans

When I was thinking about dinner-party disasters I was reminded of my mother and the French beans—one of my favourite stories. To think, there was a time before French beans!

When my parents were married, in 1951, my mother was eager to prove herself a good cook, so she asked my dad what his favourite vegetable was.

'You know, I love French beans,' he replied.

'Oh,' my mother said quietly, 'that's lovely.' In truth, she had no idea what French beans were, having been reared on cabbage and carrots and the like in her native Co. Sligo, unlike my father, who was a sophisticated Dubliner.

She decided to get advice from the vegetable man, who did the rounds of their new housing estate in his van. Helpfully, he described them to her, but he explained patiently that they were available only in summer, and it was winter, so she'd have to wait.

A few months later she spotted some long, stringy green things in the greengrocer's van and asked, 'What are they?'

'Oh, they're the French beans you asked me about,' he replied.

A light bulb lit up in Mum's head. 'How much would I need for the two of us?'

'If you had half a pound, that'd be fine,' the veg man said.

'Oh, I'll take a pound, so we can have them twice this week—he'll be delighted.' They'd just bought a new fridge, so she knew she could keep them fresh.

Dad came in for lunch at one o'clock, and she'd had his lamb chops ready, and his potatoes and carrots, as well as the French beans, so she put the plate down in front of him. He said absolutely nothing, so she was a bit taken aback: she thought he'd be terribly excited.

She sat down opposite him and said, 'Well, are you delighted?'

He was poking around on his plate and didn't seem enthusiastic, so she repeated, 'Are you not really excited, because it's your favourite veg?'

'What?' he said, pushing them around the plate, a puzzled look on his face.

'French beans,' she said. 'Your man told me to buy half a pound, and, luckily, I bought a pound, and thanks be to God I did, because half of them were empty.'

All Dad had on his plate were tiny slivers of grey-green, the result of her podding the French beans!

She's ninety-one now, and a brilliant cook.

DINNER-PARTY DISASTERS

Even if you don't pod your French beans, like my mother, you might be tempted to experiment with your dinner-party menu in order to try out a recipe from your favourite Michelin-starred restaurant. I would suggest that you do this only if you're a really competent cook. In that case your guests will probably appreciate your efforts and the results.

However, if, like me, you're just 'good enough', I think you should try to keep things as simple as you can. The last thing I want to be doing when I have guests is to be rushing in and out of the kitchen to check the temperature of the oven with a thermometer and all that nonsense.

And if you *do* have a dinner-party disaster, don't worry. If I've overcooked a leg of lamb I simply carve it onto a platter and put gravy over it, then surround it with the roast potatoes and veg. I like to call it 'family style' to disguise the fact that it's not pink. If the roast chicken isn't quite done, slice the drumsticks off and put it back in the oven. Your guests might be a bit tipsy by the time you serve it, but at least they won't have food poisoning!

In general, I think overcooking a bit is safer than under-cooking, because of the risk of making your guests ill; but if you've a complete disaster and burn the dinner to a crisp it's best just to be honest. Your guests won't mind a bit: it's you they've come to see, not your coq au vin. Either whip up a big bowl of pasta, which can be on the table in a few minutes, or smile and wave the takeaway menu!

BOTTOMS UP

I prefer to offer my guests a variety of drinks: sherry, vermouth, gin and tonic, port——classic aperitifs——although I know that not everyone has a well-stocked cocktail cabinet nowadays. Ideally, if your options are limited don't hem your guests in with prosecco: an eighteen-stone rugby player is going to look a bit strange with a glass of prosecco in his hand! How about a simple cocktail to get things started? Or a punch, which can be made with alcohol or without, for those of your guests who don't drink.

And if you'll be serving pre-dinner drinks you might like to serve some simple bites with them. To me, a canapé is something you can handle in one hand and, even more importantly, eat in one bite. There's nothing worse than trying to stuff a big canapé into your mouth or having a half-eaten one in your hand. Here are some handy one-bite items:

- Roasted baby potatoes with a dollop of crème fraîche or sour cream and snipped chives.

- Mini-profiteroles with a dab of pâté. You don't have to make your own: you can buy frozen profiteroles in supermarkets these days.

- Baby tomatoes, hollowed out and filled with cream cheese.

- Mini-samosas, bhajis or pakoras.

- Fingers of smoked salmon on brown bread.

- Tiny lamb burgers with a dab of spicy sauce.

- Satay chicken skewers. (No, not one bite, but the stick gives you something to hold onto!)

- Sliced mini-baguettes toasted and served with pâté, hummus, cream cheese—anything you fancy.

- 'Shots' of soup in little espresso cups or shot glasses.

- Little fingers of asparagus wrapped in Parma ham.

The list is endless, but it's good to have a packet of frozen pastry in the freezer. Puff pastry can be transformed into a savoury tart, which you can cut into bite-size pieces; cooked shortcrust can hold a whole range of savoury fillings; and filo can be filled with cooked prawns or feta and cooked spinach. Other handy standbys are, of course, some nice brown bread (onto which you can put smoked salmon or even cheese, if you're stuck) and any kind of creamy cheese, which can fill pastry parcels.

A NOTE ABOUT PUNCTUALITY...

A friend of mine was invited to an eightieth-birthday weekend in the country. This was in the days before mobile phones—an important point in this story! She and her husband set out from the city as soon after work as they could manage, but the traffic was terrible, and a two-hour journey turned into four. Of course, they had no way of contacting their host, and they felt that driving around looking for a phone box would only add to the delay, so they kept going.

They finally arrived, in a lather, at 9:30 p.m., only to find the entire party sitting around an empty dinner table, looking hungry and just a bit tense.

'Oh, you're here,' the host said. 'We can order at last.'

My friend was mortified to discover that everyone had arrived at 7:30 and had been sitting around for two hours waiting for her so that they could order their dinner. She had to do a lot of washing-up to make up for that faux pas!

I would say that Irish people are famous for not turning up on time at parties. There seems to be some kind of understanding that an invitation for half past seven means that you should turn up at eight, or sometimes even later. In some parts of the world being late is considered downright rude; in others it's considered positively polite. Personally, I think it really depends on your host: if they're early birds who like to go to bed at eleven they probably won't thank you for turning up to their dinner party two hours late; but if they're night owls the party will really only be getting started.

As a rule of thumb, if the invitation says, *7:30 for 8*, that generally means drinks at 7:30 and dinner at 8, and it's polite to turn up no later than 7:45. Most hosts will not be expecting you to turn up on the dot of 7:30, and indeed they might still be running around with the vacuum-cleaner. A small window of lateness is acceptable, I think. If you've a babysitter emergency, let your hosts know so that they don't sit around waiting for you. If you're hosting a dinner party and one of your guests hasn't turned up by 8:30, I think it's fine to start eating; otherwise the dinner will be burned or your guests will all be starving.

SITTING DOWN TO DINNER

When you're seating your dinner guests it's important to place people so that the conversation flows and everyone has a good time. Begin by keeping the table itself reasonably small, if you can. A huge table isn't good for a dinner party: the person on the right-hand corner can't talk to person on the left-hand corner. My brother John designs tables specifically for wedding venues, and his rule of thumb is that you should be able to touch everybody's nose with your hand. If all else fails, it will be a good dinner-party game!

Here are a few other 'rules' for seating people, which you might find useful:

- Try not to seat a husband and wife together: they'll probably be too used to talking to each other and would prefer to mingle. However, if your oldest friend has brought along their new partner, you might like to break this rule, as the partner might otherwise feel completely left out.

- Don't put two quiet people together, unless you'd like a deadly silence at that end of the table—it's good to mix your shy and chatty friends.

- If you've an odd number of diners, don't worry. Nowadays there's no need to invite an extra person to even up the numbers, and there's no need to get too hung up on mixing the sexes either.

- Don't waste your best friend, and life and soul of the party, by putting them next to you. Make the maximum use of them by putting them in the middle of the action. But if they're quiet they might like you to look after them by seating them beside you.

- As the host, you don't need to sit at the head of the table, simply somewhere convenient from where you can make your getaway to the kitchen when needed.

- If your seating plan isn't working after the main course, just mix everyone up again by suggesting that they move around.

MAKING THE TABLE SPECIAL

For many of us, time is of the essence, and you might think you haven't got time to fiddle around with flower arrangements and table settings, but simple and easy is best. A few small touches can make your dinner party look magical.

Perhaps you have an old tablecloth inherited from Granny—add some mismatched china and old wine or sherry glasses (you can often find these in charity shops) and you have a nice 'distressed' look. A few wild flowers stuffed into little jam jars at regular intervals, or lots of tea-lights in glass tumblers, can create a lovely rustic look, as can a single rose in an old teacup.

You can bring together a few different things in a theme, for example a few pretty shells or white stones, along with big chunky candles, for a beachy summer table. Or you can have a 'colour' theme, with lavender and matching napkins, or, say, a lovely, bright bunch of daffodils to go with your yellow dinner service.

And you don't have to have flowers: you can use lots of little pumpkins for an autumn table. If you want a dreamy look put a bit of tulle—that netting you see on ballerinas' dresses, which you can find in fabric shops or a florist's—around a vase and sprinkle rose petals on it, and it looks gorgeous. Or simply tie your cutlery together with a pretty ribbon on the plate. With Pinterest and other websites you won't be short of inspiration, so your theme doesn't have to be fussy or expensive.

THE ART OF DINNER-PARTY CONVERSATION

I freely admit that I talk too much and have a story about everything, so dinner parties don't present me with too many problems. Sometimes I'll be getting ready for a dinner party and I'll say to myself, 'Now, I'm not going to say a word,' and my friends think there's something wrong with me! Also, because I travel a lot and meet many people in my work, I suppose I have stories that are interesting, and people seem to enjoy them. When I meet my hotelier friends we talk hotels all the time, and it's completely boring for everyone else. Our wives and partners understand, so they just let us off, but if you have a mix of people you, as the host, just have to be careful that they're comfortable enough to talk. You have to keep the quiet person happy and draw them into the conversation as much as possible, while being respectful of their character.

As to conversation, the old 'Don't talk about religion, sex or politics' rule is probably a bit old hat: some people believe it spices things up! Others say you should avoid boring stuff like weather and work, but they're certainly safe topics to get you started. The trouble is that they don't really go anywhere, and you can end up being silent again quite soon. I always try to chat about topics that are more open-ended, such as travel, what you'd do if you won the lottery and who you'd invite, living or dead, to your ultimate dinner party. Ask 'you' questions to draw the other person out.

I came across a funny little saying by Jessica Hagy, in her book *How to Be Interesting*. 'Good conversation is a little bit like coaxing a feral cat out of a drain pipe,' she says. 'You need bait, you need something to talk about, you need to be perceived as non-threatening, and you need to prepare yourself to be hissed or clawed at.' In my experience, most people like to talk about themselves, so you can start by asking the other person questions—not too personal (!)—about themselves. Ask them how they know the host, tell them some funny story about how you got there, ask them how their week has been etc. And listen to what they say: I always think listening is actually more important than talking.

The other side of the coin is the person who just won't stop talking—a bit like myself! It's pointless to try to drown them out, so why not change the subject, or, if you're the host, suggest that they help you in the kitchen? It's your job to keep your chatty guest under control! If you're a chatterbox and are going on a bit you can take your cues from others at the table. If they've lapsed into silence while you've been holding forth it's time to quieten down a bit or to move the conversation on by asking someone else what they think.

The other thing most dinner-party hosts dread is sudden silence, punctuated only by the sound of forks scraping on plates. A compliment to the host about the food or the setting will get things moving again, or, if you dare, play devil's advocate and say something controversial about a news topic. As the host, you might like to jot down a few interesting topics from current affairs or TV that you know will get things moving again if the conversation flags. The internet provides a seemingly endless supply of daft stories and silly videos that make for great dinner-party chat.

MIND YOUR MANNERS

Hopefully by this stage in our lives most of us have half-decent table manners, but at a dinner party there are one or two crucial things to remember. Firstly, no elbows on the table. If you put your two elbows on the table you're crowding out the person beside you. Your body falls forward, your back arches slightly, and, essentially, you become a dead person at the table, blocking the conversation. There's also the possibility that you'll knock over your glass. However, after the main course, when the cutlery has been cleared away, it's fine to put one elbow on the table—we're all ready to relax by that stage.

The other big thing at dinner parties is what to do with your napkin. We no longer really use them, except at restaurants, so people might not be aware of best practice. Don't stick it in your shirt or under your tie. Instead, put it on your lap. When you've finished with it don't crumple it and toss it onto the table: leave it on your lap and then, if you're getting up, fold it and put it on the chair. Another good thing to remember is not to eat until everyone is seated and ready to start. If you grew up in a house with five brothers and sisters—where those who waited, starved—well, remember that you're not at home any more! Nobody is going to grab that last bread roll or roast potato, so you can relax and wait before you eat.

SOCIAL DRINKING

I don't drink alcohol, and some people find that hard to understand. I was at a dinner party in Adare Manor once, during a meeting on the subject of luxury hotels, and I met a lovely Scottish man called Stewart. After dinner we went out to the bar, and he asked me what I wanted to drink. I said, 'I'll have a Ballygowan,' so he turned to the barman and said, 'A double Ballygowan for Mr Brennan.' He meant well!

Needless to say, my dinner-party guests absolutely adore me for being a non-drinker, because I can drive them all home after the party; they can all be fluthered and are spared the expense of a taxi. If you'll be drinking, though, dinner parties can be tricky. You begin with pre-dinner drinks, on an empty stomach, and, before you know it, you're feeling woozy, and you haven't even eaten yet. Everyone knows their own limits, and my advice is to know when you're reaching, or going past, them. If you've had a little too much and are feeling a bit hot and bothered, don't open your tie: talk as little as possible, call a taxi and just go home. A quiet word in the host's ear is preferable to loud ramblings at the table. The next day you can send a little card saying, *Thanks for your understanding.* A friend of mine tells me that she drinks a glass of water in between every glass of wine at a dinner party. This helps her to slow down and stay hydrated—and it saves on the Andrews Liver Salts the next day!

CLEARING UP

'A good servant... avoids coughing, breathing hard, or treading on a lady's dress; never lets any article drop, and deposits plates, glasses, knives, forks and spoons noiselessly. It is now considered good form for a servant not to wear gloves in waiting at table, but to use a damask napkin, with one corner wrapped around the thumb, that he may not touch the plates and dishes with the naked hand.'—Mrs H. O. Ward, *Sensible Etiquette of the Best Society, Customs, Manners, Morals, and Home Culture* (1878)

Not too many of us have servants nowadays, or wear gloves to clear the table, so it's always nice to offer to help your host clear up, even if their answer is, 'No, thanks.' As a guest, I always offer to help, but if the host says, 'No, I'm fine,' I don't offer again, and this is my rule of thumb. I have friends who regularly host dinner parties and never accept any help clearing up. (One of their favourite sayings is from the actor Helen Carey, who was asked by an addled maid, 'Do you stack, or is you quality?') If I get up at their dinner party and even attempt to stack a plate they go mad. As far as they're concerned, my only job is to relax and enjoy the meal.

My hotel training comes out when I host a dinner party. I do all the clearing up myself, and I do it in a flash, because I'm used to it. I always think of the logistics too, such as the door in and out of the kitchen, so that you're not tripping over the guests with an armful of dirty plates. If, as a guest, I'm asked to help, I love to wash-up, because it's such a mess beforehand and so tidy afterwards. I love that effect, and I'm nowhere happier than where I can bring order to the chaos.

Washing-up always reminds me of my annual trip to Lourdes. Those of you who have taken the pilgrimage will know that the eating used to be done, until very recently, in the hall of a huge, old hospital, serving about six hundred people at a time. On one occasion it was my turn to be on washing-up duties. I worked with six great Dublin women, but they had no idea of organisation. They had all the dirty and clean plates together, and all the suds and the clean water mixed up—it was a nightmare. So I suggested that we break it all down, and we got a system going: dirty plates stacked neatly, soapy water in one place and clean water for rinsing in another, and so on. At the end of the night one woman re-marked, 'Ah, Jesus, you look as if you've done this before.' Little did she know! Such is the levelling effect of Lourdes.

THE PARTY'S OVER

I was once invited to a very posh fiftieth birthday party in the Connaught Hotel in London. The gilt-edged invitation announced that it was black tie, and it said at the bottom, *Carriages at 12*. I was so excited: after this glamorous do they were going to send us home in a carriage! At midnight we were ushered to the front door, where I learned that my 'carriage' was a taxi! I was disappointed beyond belief, but a friend later told me that that's the way you tell a guest at a posh party in London that it's time to go home.

You probably won't be able to summon carriages for your guests either, so how do you politely tell them it's time to go home? Well, it depends on where you live, I think. I live in the country, and, very often, people stay until four in the morning, but the city is different. People have babysitters and transport issues, and I think one o'clock is as late as you need to stay in anyone's house in urban areas.

Besides, parties have a natural beginning, middle and end, and it's important to observe this. I fondly remember going, as a teenager, to the home of a friend who often had birthday parties that were very popular because they had a disco. (Discos were unheard of in those days!) My friend's dad used to come in at one o'clock and say, 'That's it. Out, everyone, go home,' and we were all thrown out! It might seem rude, but his parties were always fantastic, because we were thrown out at the height of the party.

If you're a guest, wait for a certain amount of time after dessert and coffee have been served before making your move. It's not really polite to jump up straight after the tiramisu and announce that you'll be off! Also, you'll make the other guests feel they have to do the same thing, so leave a little window of time after coffee before quietly getting up and taking your leave. I always think that if it's a big party it's best not to make a song and dance about leaving, as you might start a stampede. Just sneak quietly off and call your host the next day to say you had a lovely time.

If you're the host, you'll know when you've had enough and there's no harm at all in saying, 'Now, will I call taxis?' For each person who likes to be at home at ten o'clock there's a night owl who will only be getting going at midnight, so it's fine to say you're tired and need your bed. I know people who have retired to bed and left their guests to it! And when you're saying goodbye don't spend forty minutes on the doorstep shouting and laughing: be mindful of the road where you live and of your neighbours.

SAYING THANK YOU

If you've had a fabulous time at a dinner party—and even if you haven't—a 'Thank you' is a must. Personally, I always send a card, because I think it takes effort, and people appreciate it. What I do is buy eight or ten cards at a time when I see nice ones and keep them in a drawer. There's nothing wrong, as such, with an e-mail or a text message, but it just doesn't feel right to me. An e-mail is so simple: you can do it on the bus or the Luas. But with a card you have to buy it and think of what to say and then buy a stamp and post it. You have to work at it, and it shows great respect for other people.

So, you're all set now. You're a fully fledged host and have glided smoothly through inviting guests into your lovely home, entertaining them there and being the dream guest yourself.

The people next door

'The Bible tells us to love our neighbours, and also to love our
enemies; probably because generally they are the same people.'
—G. K. Chesterton

Miss Beggs

We lived in Balally Drive when I was a child, next door to a woman called Miss Beggs, who had a magnificent garden, which she organised with military precision. On Tuesdays she'd go around with a little knife and take out the dande-lions; on Wednesdays she'd do the same with the daisies.

One day my mother spotted her and pointed to a stray daisy, saying, 'Oh, you missed one there.'

Miss Beggs replied, 'Oh, no, that's Wednesday. It's only Tuesday—I don't do that today.'

Now, Miss Beggs had a lovely skimmia tree with glorious red berries, and one year I put it to very good use. I used to make Christmas logs for sale, because my dad used to supply the Boy Scouts at Larch Hill in the Dublin Mountains with their groceries, and I'd take a few logs every time I went up with him in the van. We used to go up to the place with eighty sliced pans and that kind of thing, and I used to collect about half a dozen of the logs the scouts had chopped and make my Christmas logs with them. I'd put a hole through them with Dad's bit and brace and put a candle in the top. I'd stick on some holly with a staple gun—very ambitious in those days!—and go out with a wheel-barrow and sell the logs around the area. I made the most money ever the year Hector Gray brought in spray snow in a can, because I was able to spray my holly with it.

Anyway, disaster struck one year: there were no berries on the holly, for some reason—a shocking marketing fright for a young fellow with logs to sell! But I had noticed Miss Beggs's skimmia tree. One night, when she went to bed early, I hopped over her fence with a scissors and picked as many berries as I dared. With a little bit of fishing line I attached the red berries to the holly, and I was the only fellow in Ireland with berries on his holly. If anyone had looked closely they'd have got a fright!

When I was growing up, local communities were quite different from what they are today. There were people like Miss Beggs, but there were also plenty of mums at home, dads who would come home for lunch and kids who played on the street all day. Nowadays, with so many people out at work, the streets are a lot quieter, and, with long journeys to work, many of us hardly know our neighbours. The old networks have broken down, and people are living more isolated lives. I think the problem is particularly bad in the country: I live three-and-a-half miles from my nearest neighbour. It doesn't really bother me, because I'm rarely at home; but, for many elderly people, living alone in the country, where they may not see another human being for days on end, is a serious problem. If you live in the country, do your best to keep an eye out for your elderly neighbour.

My sister lives in a busy housing estate, and she tells me the most common problems that arise there are wheelie bins left blocking a neighbour's gate, cars being parked in front of a neighbour's house, the grass verge outside the house not being kept tidy, the front gate not being kept shut and a lot of noise being made. Any of these sound familiar? If your neighbours make you seethe, here are a few ground rules to maintain good relations.

FIVE ESSENTIALS OF BEING A GOOD NEIGHBOUR

1.

Firstly, *say hello*. In the city, where people come and go, it can be tempting to ignore the new occupant of number 25, but a cheery hello and a wave can really help. If you have a new neighbour, fill them in on bin collections and give them directions to the local shop and nearest post office or restaurant.

2.

The second big issue is *noise* and how much of it you make if you live close to your neighbour.

- Do your kids shout and roar all day long? If so, maybe you could call them in at teatime to give the neighbours' ears a rest. And there's no harm at all in asking the kids not to scream too loudly on the trampoline or not to kick the ball over the neighbours' wall. If they do, remind them to be polite when they ask for it back. We used to drive our neighbours mad by bouncing a ball against their wall for hours! We all love our children and think they're perfectly marvellous, but the elderly couple next door might not agree.

- Have you a dog that barks non-stop? I don't think there's anything more annoying than a dog left out in the garden that barks all day. If you have a dog and leave it outside while you're at work, ask your neighbours if it barks. Then you'll know to put the dog inside. If your neighbours' dog is barking all day and driving you mad, tell them nicely, as they may just not be aware of it.

This doesn't fall under the heading of noise, but if you have a dog try to keep it under control. I'm sure Miss Beggs would have been horrified if we had let a dog loose on her flowerbeds. If Fido does dig a big hole in your neighbours' rose beds, apologise and offer to pay for the damage. Also, cat and dog faeces are really unpleasant and cause huge annoyance for people, not to mention their being a health hazard. If you're taking Fido for a walk, remember to pick up after him. If your lovely cat likes weeing on the doorstep, you can buy a repellent spray, which can be got in garden centres.

- Think about the noise from your TV and radio if you live in a semi, because noise carries through the walls. The other thing to be careful about is if you have wooden floors or loud children—or indeed loud children *on* wooden floors! It's amazing how the noise can carry. Also, according to one city council in England, the noise of slamming doors is a big issue for many neighbours, so it pays to be aware of this.

- Planning a party? The first rule, as far as I'm concerned, is to tell the neighbours so that they can arrange to be elsewhere. Or, better still, invite them. If they won't be coming along, be considerate. Keep the music down if you can and switch it off at a reasonable hour: the whole estate doesn't have to be kept awake by your loud music.

- If your neighbours' loud music is driving you mad you're quite within your rights to complain, but do it politely —calling the Gardaí is probably a last resort. If your neighbours are persistently noisy, you might have to contact your local council and report it. (The other thing to bear in mind about parties is the smell—if you're having a barbecue, say. You can't really help barbie smoke wafting over the hedge into your neighbours' garden, but it's polite to let them know first—and, if you can, to invite them along.)

3.

The third ground rule of being a good neighbour is to be *careful about leaving your rubbish out*. Bins are often a flashpoint between neighbours, so it's important to keep a sense of humour about it. I came across a great website when I was researching this book, www.wheeliebinetiquette.com. It's based on an Australian neighbourhood's attempt to keep the wheelie-bin situation under control, or, as they put it, 'Keeping the lid on neighborhood (dis)content,' which really made me laugh.

You can help by leaving your wheelie bin out only the night before collection day and by taking it in as soon as it has been emptied. If you have a number of bins, tidy them into one spot and, if you can, get a cover for them to hide them away. Never put your extra rubbish in your neighbours' wheelie bin, don't leave your brown bin out for an age and don't leave your overfull bin spilling out onto the road.

4.

The fourth rule of being a good neighbour is being *considerate about your car*. In the city, parking spaces are at a premium, and people can get very hot under the collar about them. They also get very upset about commuters parking on their street and then taking the bus into town——an increasingly common problem.

Thankfully, I don't have to worry too much about parking in my remote part of the world, but according to an article I read in the *Daily Mail* ('Parking rage'), in busy areas, where on-street parking is the only option, people can resort to extreme measures to keep their parking space, such as putting traffic cones down in front of their house and blocking the space with their wheelie bins. Apparently, according to a survey conducted by the insurance company Direct Line, 10 per cent of the 2,500-odd people who responded admitted to having retaliated, if a neighbour parked in their spot, by blocking their car. Others left angry notes on each other's windscreens, and some have even gone so far as to move house because of parking difficulties.

If you're parking in a city locality and travelling into town, try to be considerate of the local people. Many city areas are plagued by commuters leaving their cars parked there all day, reducing driving safety and bringing down the general feel of the area. If this is the case in your area, your local council may be able to help by placing double yellow lines and other deterrents, so get in touch with the relevant department.

At home, try to park only in front of your own house or in your driveway, not half in front of your neighbours' house. I also think that if you're having problems with parking it's really best to just talk to your neighbour. The silent war of the note on the windscreen is probably not the best way to go about things, and you might very well find a solution if you both communicate. Try not to let things get out of hand if you have a parking dispute with your neighbour: once things get 'official' it's very difficult to row back.

In the countryside, of course, you're unlikely to have parking disputes, so it's all the more important that you look out for your neighbours, particularly these days, when elderly people in the country can be very isolated. Don't be like the neighbours I heard about in America recently who didn't realise their neighbour had died—six years previously! Try to look out for your neighbours: offer to take in their post, mind their cat or water their garden while they're on holiday, or hold a spare key for them. If they're elderly, drop in every so often to check that things are okay. Many of us think we haven't got the time nowadays, but the benefits are great for them and for you.

I'm reminded here of my mother's neighbour. She's ninety-one and lives alone, but she makes regular trips to her local chemist's for her prescription. On one occasion the members of staff noticed that she wasn't looking very well and suggested that she sit down. It turned out that she was having a heart attack, and they had to call an ambulance. It just goes to show: keeping in touch with your neighbour or community can be an absolute life-saver.

Needless to say, looking out for your neighbour does not mean being nosy! No peeking at their post to see how much tax they're paying!

5.

The fifth and final rule of being a good neighbour is to *be considerate about building work.* This begins with planning permission, which so many people get upset about. Even if you think your neighbour is going to object, talk to them anyway and you'll know then that you tried your best to keep the lines of communication open. The same applies to having work done on your home. If you'll need to put up a hoarding to keep dust and dirt out of your neighbours' home, make sure to tell them. I'm sure they'll be only delighted not to have a house covered in dust.

It's also important not to put your skip in front of their driveway and to let them know in advance if there will be any particularly loud noises or big machines involved. Many neighbours do get upset about building work and that kind of disruption, so it's best to consider things from their point of view and to chat with them about any potential areas of difficulty. You don't want things to get out of hand, particularly when it comes to legal action, as it's very hard to find a way back from that. Try to resolve all disputes amicably first. The same goes for repairs to your property, overhanging trees and hedges, rubbish, toys in the front garden and that kind of thing.

MAKING YOUR LOCAL AREA A BETTER PLACE

Of course, quite apart from learning to live next door to your neighbours, you might find it rewarding to become more involved in your local area. If you live in the city you can take part in, or organise, street-cleaning every so often. Your local council provides the bags and the tools, and you organise a gang to clean up. It can be a great way of getting to know your neighbours.

You can also talk to your local council about planting in open spaces. Many areas now have lovely plants on grass verges and green spaces, as well as other community initiatives, such as small local festivals and 'street feasts' (www.streetfeast.ie), where local groups organise a street or garden party to get the community together.

THE WIDER COMMUNITY

My nearest town is Kenmare, and I go there for Mass and to buy little bits and pieces. Every time I do I'm struck by how important the local community is. In my area the GAA is fantastic for children and adults alike, because it builds a true community spirit. There's nothing like the place on match day, when all the colours are on display. What would we do without the GAA!

Whether you live in the middle of nowhere, in a little town or in the city, you'll be part of a community, using community services: the local post office, hairdresser, café, taxi service and supermarket. Maybe you live in an estate and travel to work in a city fifty miles away, returning only in the evening. Well, you still use council services, possibly a local crèche, your local garage or shop and the local café for breakfast on a Saturday morning. Even if you don't spend a lot of time there, you're part of the place in which you live, and you need to get along with the local people, and they with you. This means being polite when asking for service and tipping and queueing properly.

Isabel and the biscuits

I love local cafés. They can be a great place to people-watch, and popping in to one always reminds me of my friend Isabel. I was in university with her in Cathal Brugha Street, and she is a lovely woman, if a bit scattered. She was always late for lectures, and this was in the days when you were monitored and given a warning if you were late. This particular day she slept through her alarm, so she had to jump on her bike, pedal like fury into Cathal Brugha Street, throw her coat into her locker and run to the lecture theatre. When she got there she found it empty: it was Tuesday; she had no lectures. She'd thought it was Wednesday.

'Well, I'm going to treat myself after killing myself getting in here,' Isabel said to herself, and off she went into Bewley's on Grafton Street, locking her bike to a railing outside. She bought a packet of Snack biscuits—the yellow one with the six biscuits in it (this is important!)—and a cup of tea and scouted around for a table. They were all taken, so she realised she'd have to share one. She went over to a table where a man was sitting and asked if it was okay to sit there. When he said yes she pulled out the chair and began to take off her coat and sit down. 'Thank God,' she thought, 'for a bit of a rest.'

As she took her seat, she was astonished to see the man reach out and take her packet of biscuits, opening it and helping himself to one. She thought, 'My God, the cheek of him,' but decided not to say anything: she just took the packet back and had a biscuit. He then pulled it back over to himself and took another biscuit!

Isabel was beginning to get more than a bit annoyed at this stage, when the man got up and went over to the counter to get a cup of coffee. He bought a doughnut with cream and jam and then scanned the room before sitting down as far away from Isabel as he could get.

Isabel was incredulous. 'The nerve,' she thought. 'He's after eating my biscuits, then he moves table. Well, I'm going to give him a bit of a fright!'

She got up and put on her coat, hat and bag, and as she was walking past his table she reached out and grabbed his doughnut and took a big bite out of it. She plopped it down on the plate, cream shooting out of it, and said, 'Now!' before walking out, delighted with herself. 'It served him right, after eating my biscuits,' she grumbled to herself as she went to unlock her bike. 'Some people have no manners at all,' she thought, looking in her pockets for her keys. And what did she find? Her packet of Snack biscuits. She'd been eating his all along!

CAFÉ SOCIETY

I hope you won't take a leaf out of Isabel's book when you're in a café and will instead eat your own food. But there are a few other little things you might need to be aware of. Sitting in a café means that you'll be close to other people, so it's important to remember this. Try not to have loud conversations, to listen to music that can be heard through your earphones or to hog tables when there are a lot of people waiting. Some people don't like sharing tables with strangers at busy times, but I really don't mind. I don't think you can expect to hang on to a table for four if you're by yourself at lunchtime, biscuits or no biscuits. If there's an Isabel at large, you can just hide your slice of cake! Even if your local café isn't the Ritz, the same rules apply: manners at all times.

There's a new twist nowadays to café society. Because many cafés offer wireless internet access, it can be tempting to stay around all day, particularly if you're self-employed. But how long is too long to linger over a cup of coffee? According to *BBC News Magazine* it's called 'e-freeloading', sitting for five hours over one cup of coffee so that you can use the wi-fi. And apparently it's not just coffee shops, as I learned from this little snippet in the magazine, which made me laugh: 'There's currently a pseudo turf war in New York between McDonald's staff and a group of Korean senior citizens, who apparently spend all day sharing one portion of chips.'

There's no hard and fast rule when it comes to lingering: some people feel that if they've paid almost three euro for a coffee they're entitled to stay for a good while, and some coffee chains have a policy of leaving customers alone. But the consensus seems to be that you should buy something every hour if you're spending all day in a café, that is, if it's your 'coffice', to quote the *Huffington Post*.

In fact, there's a new idea in café culture now according to which everything is free—tea, coffee, buns, etc.—but you pay by the minute for the time and the wi-fi. I think it's a brilliant idea. I read about a café opening in London that charges three pence a minute for the time spent, and you can bring your own biccies. A plus for the Isabels of this world...

TIPPING

In the United States, where I travel a lot, tipping is a way of life. They tip everyone, including chambermaids, bellboys and hairdressers. All the bills have 10, 15 and 20 per cent tip calculations already on them, so it makes it very easy to tip. If you've had very good service you can give 20 per cent; if the service has been fine, 15; and just okay, 10.

Tipping is not hugely in the psyche of Irish people, really, possibly because until quite recently we didn't have the extra cash—or, indeed, that many places to spend it in. But I think it should be, because the workers are often on a low wage. I generally aim to give about 15 per cent of the bill, and 10 as a minimum. I always tip taxi-drivers and hairdressers, and I try to remember the Saturday young woman or man who does the hair-washing, as they get paid so little.

I never don't tip, but if I'm not happy with the service I don't leave a ton. I know, some people think that not tipping at all is fair enough if the service has been poor, but I think it's a bit harsh. I generally leave cash as a tip. The days are probably gone when waiters didn't receive the gratuity added to the customer's bill, but leaving cash ensures that the waiter, busboy or chambermaid will get the money.

COMPLAINING NICELY

Of course, there are times in life when you'll need to complain about the service in a café or shop. Some people would rather die than complain; others will moan about everything from the olives on the table to the potpourri in the bathroom.

I was in a seafood restaurant in Texas on a business trip once when a fellow customer complained to the waitress that the topping on his lobster was cold. (I know, would that we all had that kind of problem!) The waitress said, 'Oh, I'm terribly sorry. Will I change your lobster or your topping?' This nice young woman offered to replace a whole lobster for the customer, who, after saying yes, then refused to eat it. Can you imagine! He said he wasn't happy, even though his two sons were happily gorging away, and when the waitress offered to send the manager over—a woman called Alison—he said, 'I didn't come here to talk to Alison.' I felt like saying, 'You'd want to get a bit of sense in life, quite honestly.' This is clearly an example of how not to complain!

I have to say that I think Irish people are terrible for complaining, meaning that we don't do enough of it, and when we do we get it all wrong. We either rant and rave or go about it in such a roundabout way that the staff don't even realise we're complaining.

In the hotel business, we're well used to people complaining, and we have a bit of a rule: the ruder you are to us, the nicer we get. Then you have less and less to be rude about.

Here's a good example. We had a group checking in at the Park once. They'd booked fifteen rooms initially and had then changed their minds a few times about numbers, before we eventually managed to squeeze them all in—into twenty-five rooms, in the end, including a small single room that we wouldn't normally use. The man who got this room wasn't at all happy about it and came marching up to the reception desk. 'Who's in charge here?' he demanded. When I said it was me he announced, 'I'm not happy with my room: my bathroom is tiny.'

I explained that we wouldn't normally use that room, but because the group was so large, and we wanted to fit everyone in, we'd had no choice.

He looked at me and said, 'Do you know that in my house I have eleven bathrooms and none of them is that size?'

I replied, 'Oh, eleven bathrooms?'

'Eleven bathrooms,' he repeated, poking me on the shoulder for emphasis.

I said, 'And in my house I have forty-seven bathrooms.'

There was a moment's silence and then he started to die laughing. He knew he'd been outwitted. It all goes to show, you can diffuse what could be a big problem by being nice but straight. And you can make a complaint with a bit more tact than my friend. Here are a few tips:

COMPLAINING

1.

Begin quietly. If you're in a café and the waiter forgets your cappuccino order, don't click your fingers and yell: catch their eye and gently remind them. If your soup is cold, quietly ask if it could be replaced. Your goal is to get hot soup, not to humiliate people in public.

2.

It's best not to fume for the whole meal if there's a problem with your starter. Try to deal with any problem quickly.

3.

Try not to be personal: 'Are you being deliberately slow with my coffee?' Keep it neutral and focus on the issue, not the person.

4.

Have a little think about how you want the problem to be resolved. Do you want your poor main course replaced or do you want a reduction in your bill because of it? Many restaurants will offer this automatically, but if they don't, just ask politely.

5.

If the waiter doesn't deal with your complaint, ask to speak to the manager. Explain what the problem is and how you think it can be resolved. Most restaurants will be only too happy to make their customers happy; but, if not, you're not obliged to pay a tip. If the problem is a serious one, such as poor hygiene, you can complain to your environmental health officer, at your local council. And remember, most restaurants rely on recommendations, so they won't want an unhappy customer spreading the word that their establishment isn't up to scratch!

6.

If your complaint relates to poor service in the local dry-cleaners, for example, it's important that you know your rights, and you can find out more about these on the Consumers' Association of Ireland website, www.thecai.ie. The old saying 'The customer is always right' doesn't necessarily apply in the way it once did. With so many purchases being made online, consumers—that's you—have to be careful to read the small print and to know exactly what it is they have ordered. Take internet bookings, for example, which we frequently receive at the hotel. They're impersonal, and it's often not clear to customers what they've booked. People can become quite irate when they discover that their booking doesn't include breakfast, for instance. For more information on consumer rights and online booking, have a look at 'Complaining online' in Chapter 9 (p. 211).

QUEUEING

I read recently that queueing etiquette is to form part of the citizenship test in Britain, which goes to show you how seriously they take the whole business. Some people, it has to be said, think that queueing is a kind of sport. You'll know who these people are by the fact that they're looking at the rest of the queue, waiting for their cue, if you'll excuse the pun, to jump. Well, a queue is a queue, as far as I'm concerned. Jumping a queue goes against the whole concept of fairness, as well as being just maddening.

I always think that it pays to **be quick when you're in a queue**. My whole aim is to get my job done and get away quickly. Because I travel a lot, I'm always ready at airport security. I have my clear plastic bag with my toiletries in it; I have my shoes open and my laptop out. If there's a confused-looking elderly couple I always explain to them what they have to do. The same goes for any queueing: the usual queueing rules don't apply to some older people, because it can just take them longer to find what they need and to fish out the right change. If you get impatient just imagine if this was your mother and she had a stranger breathing down her neck to get a move on!

That's the next rule of queueing: *try not to barge ahead*. If you're in the post office and you're not sure where the queue ends, just ask the person at the end, 'Is there a queue here?' and take your place. I try not to stand too close to the person in front, as I like to respect other people's personal space. And try not to ask a friend to save your place while you nip out to the car for something: other queuers hate it, which is understandable. The same goes for asking a friend to nab a table for you in a café while you go up to the counter: you might avoid the busy lunchtime queues, but you probably won't be very popular. And if you can pay attention to the annoying automated system in the post office—'Counter number 9, please' —it really helps, as you can keep the queue moving.

In the supermarket, some of us can get into a bit of a state about *packing our bags*, because the checkout operator seems to scan our groceries so quickly. Before we know it we have a big pile of things to pack away and only thirty seconds to do it in. If this is you, don't panic. I try to scoot to the end of the checkout with my bag ready, so that I can pack as the operator scans. If you're slower, avail of the packing assistance some supermarkets offer, or just pack your things quickly back into your trolley and then find a quiet place to pack once you've paid.

If you do notice someone who is slow, *offer to help them*: 'Can I help you to pack?' I'm sure they'll be only delighted. And if you feel yourself getting hot under the collar, try not to huff and puff with impatience when someone isn't getting a move on, or to mutter under your breath. Life is so fast these days that it doesn't do any harm to slow down from time to time. Ask yourself what you'll really gain by being thirty seconds faster at the checkout.

MANNERS FOR DAILY LIFE

In our daily lives many of us have to remember our manners in lots of different situations: in a queue, holding a door open for someone, giving up a seat for an elderly person—that kind of thing. My rule of thumb is 'Everybody is my mother, and how would I like her to be treated?' (Having said that, I once offered my seat to a woman on the Tube in London, and she nearly ate me alive! 'What do you mean? We're of equal status, and I don't need to sit down!' she told me. I was mortified!)

Holding a door open for someone can be another grey area. Of course, when you go through a door, you don't want to let it swing back on the person behind you, but neither do you want to stand there for ten minutes waiting for that person, who then feels they have to start running in order not to hold you up. There's a happy medium between holding the door and just letting it go. It needs to be judged case by case, but always look behind you to check. (Recently I was at the theatre, and a woman was coming out through a set of double doors with her husband, who was in a wheelchair. I opened the first set of doors for her to let him through, but suddenly another man crashed in through the first door, blocking the wheelchair. He thought I was keeping it open for him!) The whole chivalrous notion of the man holding the door open for the woman is probably old hat now, but maybe we should hold the door open for others as a matter of course.

If you're in a *queue in the post office* and you see an elderly person or a parent with a young child, why not let them in ahead of you? It's not a race, and they'll be only too delighted not to have to struggle with buggies and that kind of thing. The same goes for supermarket trolleys: offer to help elderly people with them, because they often find them hard to manage.

If you're *getting into a lift* it's nice to greet the person already in it with a polite 'Hello,' but you don't need to tell them your life story. And if you're getting into a lift with a friend, consider not continuing your conversation at a yell: keep it quiet or save it for later.

Last, but not least, remember the 'magic words', as Emily Post calls them—the words that your mother taught you and that will make your daily interactions go so much more smoothly:

'PLEASE'

and

'THANK YOU'!

The big occasions:

'The capacity for friendship is God's way
of apologising for our families.'
—Jay McInerney

The bull in the bed

I hope this won't be too irreverent a way of introducing a chapter on the major events in life, but one of my favourite funeral stories is the one of the bull in the bed in Carrick-on-Shannon.

Friends of ours had a B&B there in the 1970s. It was a big success, and they kept extending and extending it, adding a bedroom here and a bedroom there, until they reached the thirty-foot cliff that lay behind the house and could go no further. There was a bull in the field at the top of the cliff, which will be relevant to this story…

Sadly, the family's father died suddenly on Holy Saturday, and there was consternation in the house. The B&B was to host a bridal party on Easter Monday—in those times, you couldn't have a wedding during Lent, so the first day on which you could hold one would be Easter Monday—which would clash with the funeral. The bridal group was to turn up on the Monday, and the family would be going to the church for the removal at five o'clock.

On that Saturday afternoon, despite the consternation, the mother decided she needed to check the rooms to make sure they were okay for the bridal party, and when she went down and opened the bedroom door, what should she find but a bull in the bed! A very *angry* bull!

No, it's not a joke! What had happened was that he'd broken the fence on the cliff above and had fallen through the flat roof, which he'd demolished, and had come straight down into the bedroom. He was perfectly fine—but raging, needless to say! The problem was that he was too wide to get out the door. As well as that, the father's body was being removed that night, and so the family had to go down to the church, in hysterics crying at his death, but also laughing at the bull in the bed. They had to put the bridal couple in another room—I can only imagine what excuse they made—and on Tuesday afternoon, after the funeral Mass, they got the vet to sedate the animal, and a carpenter to remove the door jamb, and the bull was carried out the bedroom door, up the hall and out the front door.

It's true that laughter and tears can coexist on even the most tragic of occasions.

Most of us are unlikely to encounter a bull in the bed in our lifetime, but it's certainly true that, in our informal world, there are really only three properly formal occasions left: the 'hatches, matches and despatches' that are the milestones in our lives. Gliding smoothly through all the protocols involved can often be a challenge. What's more, we'll be spending time with our family, which for some of us isn't always easy. Even if we get on famously with our nearest and dearest, a formal event, such as a wedding, can put a strain on any relationship, and there's nothing like an occasion on which a few glasses of champagne are mixed with high emotion to get the fireworks started...

BEGIN AT THE BEGINNING

I think there's truly nothing more marvellous than a new arrival into the world. It's a uniquely happy event. Even at weddings, you can get grumbling about overdoing it, silly presents and 'Bridezillas', but births bring out the joy for everyone.

Nowadays the first you hear about a birth is probably a text message from a delighted dad (Mum being too tired to send it), and he'll often put pictures of the baby up on the internet or e-mail them to friends and family. It's all very informal, and it's lovely to see pictures of the baby straight away. However, I still like the old-fashioned way——receiving a birth-announcement card in the post——as it makes a wonderful memento for the parents and those who receive it. Normally the wording is as follows:

> Jim and Mary Murphy [if you don't share a name you can simply put 'Jim Murphy and Mary O'Brien…' etc.] are pleased to announce the birth of their baby girl, Grace, at X [name of hospital here, or 'at home'], on 21 September 2014, weighing 8 lb 2 oz. [After this you can mention the baby's siblings, if there are any.]

Some people also like to put a birth announcement in the paper, particularly if they're living abroad. It may seem a wee bit old-fashioned to some, but, again, it's a lovely memento that Granny and Granddad can cut out of the paper and keep. If you want to put an announcement in the paper, the wording is slightly different: it begins with the family name or names, as appropriate, followed by the baby's name——specifying the surname if the couple haven't got the same names——the date of birth and whether the baby is a sibling. Here's an example:

> MURPHY, Jim and Mary (née O'Brien), are delighted to announce the birth of a daughter, Grace Margaret, on 21 September 2014, a sister for Gemma.

Or:

MURPHY and O'BRIEN. Jim and Mary are delighted to announce the birth of a daughter, Grace Margaret O'Brien, on 21 September...

Some parents like to add a note of thanks to the hospital or to mention the proud grandparents.

A much-loved grandchild to Betty and Brian Murphy and to Pat and Jenny O'Brien. Sincere thanks to the staff at X hospital.

THE PERFECT PRESENTS FOR A NEW BABY

People are often a bit confused about what presents to get for a new baby. Pink or blue? Pretty clothes that the baby will grow out of in a month, or something a little bit more permanent? Online companies will have plenty of ideas for baby presents. (I was highly entertained to see one website offering a set of flashcards for your newborn—there's nothing like getting an early start!) I always look for something a little different and special that will last Baby a lifetime. I was in South America once and got beautiful blown-glass angels with gold leaf through them—a special little present for someone. I know that nowadays not everyone is religious with a capital R, but, personally, I like a christening present to be spiritual, because it marks a child's beginning in life. By this I don't mean Catholic or any specific religion: a guardian angel is for everybody.

Many people like to stick to the tradition of giving a baby something silver. Like many of our traditions, giving silver napkin rings and mugs comes from Victorian times, but the idea of the present in silver comes, I'm told, from the Middle Ages, when the wealthier classes had silver spoons made for themselves, rather than the wooden ones of the humble peasant—hence the expression 'born with a silver spoon in their mouth'!

In Ireland a prize bond is another popular present, as, indeed, is a silver dollar, which used to come from relatives in America. The trick here is to choose something personal: a friend of mine worked in an office, and the tea lady used to knit every new arrival an Aran jumper. They were all delighted at the lovely handmade present, and their children wore them with pride.

Of course, if you don't knit, or if you don't want to buy silver, a painting suitable for a child's room (perhaps by a local artist), a china plate and bowl with a suitable baby motif on it, or a lovely hand-knitted baby blanket would be lovely. I think anything that can be kept as a lifelong memento is perfect.

CHRISTENINGS AND NAMING CEREMONIES

The next milestone for many new parents is the baby's christening or naming ceremony. In days gone by, particularly for Catholics, a christening or baptism was generally held when the baby was a couple of weeks old, and the religious aspects of the tradition were hugely important. Nowadays, of course, that has changed. We live in a more secular society, and one with people of many faiths in it. But, whatever the tradition, many people still like to mark the arrival of their new baby into the world. A growing minority also like to celebrate it by having a naming day for their son or daughter. Generally, parents now wait until their baby is a few months old before having any kind of a ceremony.

A traditional religious service, followed by a lunch, is still the favoured route for many parents, and if this is your choice it's nice to begin by inviting everyone in writing. I think a personalised card really makes the occasion special, even in the days of social media, and it will be a memento too. You'll see lots of companies online that offer a printing service for your cards, and your invitation might contain the following wording:

Jim and Mary Murphy
invite you to witness the christening of
Grace Margaret Murphy
at the Church of the Holy Name, Rathmurphy
On 12 July 2014 at 11 a.m.
Lunch after at [home or hotel address]
RSVP Mary Murphy, 087 xxx xxxx

If you'll be having a naming ceremony you might word your invitation as follows:

Jim and Mary Murphy
invite you to join in the naming ceremony of
Grace Margaret Murphy
at [home or venue address]
On 12 July 2014 at 11 a.m.
RSVP Mary Murphy, 087 xxx xxxxx

Whether going the traditional or non-traditional route, parents like to nominate responsible adults, who will take a lifelong interest in their child, as godparents. This is sometimes a tricky thing: your best friend from the office might not be your best friend in twenty years' time, or they may turn out to be not that great at the job. Many parents like to select family members as godparents, which I suppose ensures that they can't back out of their responsibilities! It also ensures that one friend won't be chosen over another, with the upset that that can cause.

If you've been chosen to be a godparent to a friend's or relative's baby it's an honour, and you should try to be an attentive godparent, never forgetting birthdays, Communions, Confirmations or any other milestones in your charge's life. I'm a godfather to three young people, and I've really enjoyed doing my bit. I haven't forgotten any significant occasions, but the age of twenty-one is my cut-off point, as they're grown up by then, and I think all good things must come to an end. When your charge reaches that age your work as a godparent is done!

A wedding in French

Another rite of passage in life, the wedding, has assumed fairly elaborate proportions nowadays, with all kinds of new traditions added to the day itself——not to mention stag and hen weekends, after-wedding barbecues and that kind of thing. It's also more complex socially, with people from a range of backgrounds and lifestyles attending. Of course, there's also the civil partnership ceremony, a new celebration. Nonetheless, many of the old traditions remain. It's a formal occasion, as well as a family one, and, as anyone will tell you, it's also a feat of organisation!

One of my favourite wedding stories involves my old friend Father Martin, who is a priest in London. Some years ago he was assigned to a French-speaking parish there, and the church was attended by many refugees and French-speaking Africans. Father Martin didn't speak a word of French, so he was sent off to Belgium to the nuns for a six-month French course. He graduated accordingly, but he'd lost a lot of weight, because they don't eat like the Irish, as he discovered!

His job was a difficult one, as many of his parishioners were traumatised and stressed, and in many cases the French they spoke was in a different dialect. It was all quite a worry for Father Martin. He'd been there only three weeks when the parish priest announced that they were all away the following weekend and that Father Martin was on his own. And he had a wedding to do. He was absolutely terrified and spent the next week composing his sermon in his head.

Another one of his jobs was to feed sixty to seventy homeless people, giving them sandwiches and soup every lunchtime. The rule was that whichever priest was to serve the lunchtime crowds had to go round the local restaurants to see if they were getting rid of any sandwiches. If not, the priest had to make a little trip to the supermarket.

On the morning of the wedding, Father Martin got up and went off round all the sandwich places in the area, but with no luck: there wasn't a sandwich to be found. So he had to resort to the supermarket, where he bought ham and a dozen sliced pans, lugging them back to the parish centre in big plastic bags. He rounded the corner into the street where the church was and saw that a huge crowd had gathered outside it. He thought, 'Oh, my goodness, there must be a fire or something dreadful.'

He began to panic a bit, but then one of his parishioners came up to him and said, 'Hello, Martin.' He didn't have the look of a man in an emergency. And then Father Martin saw another parishioner, who was very dressed up. It turned out that it was 12:50, and they were all outside the church for the wedding at one o'clock. He had to make a hundred rounds of sandwiches for the homeless people and do a wedding at the same time——in French!

WEDDINGS AND CIVIL PARTNERSHIPS

INVITATIONS

Unless you're Father Martin, you'll have done your planning long in advance, and often the first symbol of the wedding is the invitation or, these days, a 'save the date' card, which announces that a wedding will be held on a certain date. This can be very useful, now that wedding venues need to be booked far in advance, and it allows the bride and groom to plan ahead. I read about a save-the-date 'e-vite' when I was doing my research, which I didn't really like the sound of! I know, it's a practical solution, but I think there are a few occasions when the old-fashioned way is the most special, and this is one of them.

Weddings are probably the only remaining occasion for which an invitation is essential, and they tend to be quite tra-ditional in format. I know it might sound outmoded, but the usual way to address an invitation is to refer to the couple by the man's name, and I always do this——'Mr and Mrs John Brown'. It's true that when I'm addressing the envelope I think, 'There's nobody really doing this any more,' but I grew up at a time when this was the done thing. If the couple aren't married, the form 'Ms Mary Brennan' is fine.

It's also true that the invitations used to come from the parents of the bride. You'll probably remember the wording:

Mr and Mrs Eddie Murphy request the honour of
your presence at the marriage of their daughter
Chloe to Mr Clarence O'Brien at the Church of the
Holy Name, Rathdown, on 12 July 2014 at 1 p.m.

However, many invitations now come from the bride and groom:

Chloe Murphy and Clarence O'Brien invite you to
share in their wedding at the Church of the Holy
Name… [This will be followed by 'and afterwards at
the Bay Hotel, Baytown' and then an RSVP in the
bottom left-hand corner, with an address to reply to.]

The sending of wedding invitations can sometimes be a bit of a social minefield now that people have all kinds of different life situations: maybe they're divorced, separated or unmarried. If you're sending an invitation to an office colleague, say, and you're unsure of their partner's name, try not to put 'plus one' or 'and guest' if you possibly can. There's no problem at all in asking your colleague for their partner's name in order to add it to the invitation, in which case you'll use the form 'Mr John Murphy and Ms Mary O'Brien' and address it accordingly. They'll probably be delighted that you went to the trouble of asking.

The same goes if your guest is divorced or separated. There's no harm at all in asking politely how they'd like you to address their invitation: they'll be grateful for your consideration. If your guest has a same-sex partner you can word it like this: 'Mr John Murphy and Mr Jim O'Brien'. And if your guest is single and will be coming alone, just use their name alone on the invitation: 'Mr John Murphy' or 'Ms Mary O'Brien'.

Replying to invitations isn't quite the event it used to be, because most wedding invitations nowadays will include a reply card, which you can just return. It used to be the norm to reply in a square block centred on an A4 page: 'Mr Francis Brennan is delighted to attend the wedding of… and will be with you on X date'. This was the proper way to do it when I was growing up. I can't remember when I did it last; it's a quaint tradition, but you might find that the older generation appreciate it.

WEDDING PRESENTS

My mother and father were married for thirty-seven years, and the ivory-handled bread knife my mother used every day of her life was given to her as a wedding present. If she said it once, she said it a million times: 'This bread knife was a present from…' It used to drive us mad! But I can't help thinking that it's nice that a wedding present should last so long and have that kind of meaning. I always try to give something that has a presence and will last a lifetime. If you give them a toaster it'll be practical, but it'll be gone in a year or two.

The modern tradition of giving money is something that takes a little getting used to, although I suppose the custom of the dowry is as old as the hills. In other cultures giving money is still very much part of tradition. I was in Egypt in 1987, staying at the Hilton Hotel, where a wedding was taking place. The bride and groom were put on a kind of cake stand, and everyone went up and pinned money on them, which I found fascinating. In China wedding guests fill a red envelope—a *hóngbāo*—with a present of money for the bride and groom.

In the western world, where the giving of physical presents is the norm, the practice of asking for money at weddings has begun to creep in. I suppose it's understandable, as weddings these days cost such a lot. Mind you, I was a bit surprised when a couple of American friends of mine sent me an invitation, because they were getting married in Washington. In the invitation was a 'registry', or wedding list, for a popular American shop. I'm not wild about lists, as you tend to get left with the 42-inch television, but I was astonished to see at the bottom of the list: 'or checks can be sent to the following account.' I gave her an Irish linen tablecloth. And even though, sadly, she got divorced some time later, she still has the tablecloth!

Unlike with christening presents, I think it's a good idea to keep wedding presents fairly neutral. It's easy to get carried away with cheesy bride-and-groom figurines or his 'n' hers towels, but such presents might not be to their taste! If you're unsure about what to get a couple, and they haven't provided a list, suitable wedding presents might include:

- An *antique carving set* or *antique cutlery*. These are often not as expensive as new canteens and can be found at antique fairs. You can also find a set of pretty, antique silver teaspoons or antique lace tablecloths or napkins, which all make lovely presents.

- A *Waterford Crystal decanter* used to be a very popular choice. Nowadays people tend not to like crystal quite so much——I suppose they don't need to keep the sherry in them——so you could find a nice modern carafe or jug and matching glass set.

- A *painting*, although you have to be careful that it would be to their taste.

- A *voucher for their favourite restaurant or hotel* makes a nice alternative to a voucher for a department store, and the couple would be more likely to use it.

- I've seen a lovely *personalised wedding newspaper*, with the bride and groom's story and nice features about them. It can be ordered online, as can any number of personalised wedding presents.

- Thanks to the wonders of the internet, you can *order lovely things online* from the Museum of Modern Art in New York, for example for the art lovers in your life, or from a trendy Swedish design house, or indeed from Irish craft companies. The world is your oyster, and you'll be guaranteed to please the bride and groom with something different.

If you're the bride and groom and have received an unwanted present, you may very well be able to return it: most presents come with receipts, or perhaps you might consider donating it to charity.

SPEECHES

You've turned up in your best cocktail dress and hat to your friend's wedding, having bought the perfect present. You've enjoyed the champagne and the lovely dinner, and, at last, you can relax and listen to the speeches. And then the best man makes an off-colour speech, or the bride's father drones on for half an hour...

The whole area of speeches is fraught with difficulty and frayed nerves. As far as I'm concerned, the rule of thumb is to remember that it's a formal family occasion and, more importantly, that you'll have guests of all ages attending, so you'll need to pitch speeches accordingly—but you'll also need to have fun.

For example, my brother John was best man at a friend's wedding, and during his speech he alluded to his friend's former 'wild lifestyle', which brought the house down, and he even invited two women, who were in on the joke, to come to the top of the room and return the keys to the groom's Dublin flat! For the rest of the wedding, people were quietly wondering how the groom had managed to conceal an apartment in Dublin. It was a risqué speech, but it was designed to make the adults laugh and to go right over the children's heads.

I think risqué is fine at a wedding speech, but lewd isn't, and it can often be a fine line. It's quite acceptable to allude to a former life of late nights and partying if you don't get specific about it. If you're making a speech, be careful about the kind of incidents you plan to mention. Perhaps do your speech in front of a friend before the wedding, as they'll be able to judge if it's overdone in any way—no slide show with the groom or bride misbehaving on holiday. Warmth and affection is the way to go, and I would avoid any fond mentions of serious boyfriends or girlfriends past!

The length of your speech is also very important, and I think you should keep to ten minutes as a maximum. Some people are brilliant at stories and speaking, but if you're dying a death, as so many of us do, just keep it short and sincere. It's also very important to prepare your speech in advance and to practise it, to ensure that you've remembered to acknowledge everyone. There are any number of little books available on wedding speeches, so if you've any qualms buy one and use it—it will have sample speeches, tips for speech protocols and a list of people to thank, so that you don't leave the mother of the bride out!

If you don't feel comfortable with jokes, just aim for short humorous asides or anecdotes, not long, rambling ones, whose punchline you'll inevitably forget. And try to deliver your speech slowly: if you're not a natural performer it will be tempting to speed through it to get it over with; but remember, the bride and groom will really appreciate your speech if they can hear it properly.

It's also useful to remember who you're expected to toast in your speech: the father of the bride toasts the bride and groom, the groom toasts the bridesmaids, and the best man toasts the bride and groom.

DRESS CODES FOR FORMAL OCCASIONS

People get in a bit of a flap about dress codes when it comes to big occasions, but I think that if you follow the general rule of being respectful to the occasion you can't go too far wrong. Also, the time of day will usually influence dress codes. For a christening or Holy Communion you can be a little bit less formal, because the event is earlier in the day. For men, a jacket with an open-necked shirt is fine; for women, a smart dress. For children, smart jeans and shirts or dresses are fine. Nobody expects a child to wear a suit and tie. Mum and Dad should present properly, and guests can be a little bit less formal. (The exception to this rule is if you're visiting Buckingham Palace for morning coffee with the Queen, in which case women will need a suit and hat, and men a grey morning suit with grey pinstripe trousers and a straight tie. In case you need to know…)

There are a number of dress codes in operation in western countries, including white tie, 'business casual' and a whole lot of others. The list is a long one, but I've narrowed it down to a few essentials:

BLACK TIE

For men, this means a tuxedo, shirt and bow tie (not a straight tie, which you see all over the place now; Brad Pitt and others have made this popular, but we'll do it right or not at all!). The black tuxedo would feature a black dinner jacket and a black trouser with silk stripe. I don't believe in any colour other than black for ties, and black shoes go with a tuxedo. (See below for a nice story!)

For women, the dress can vary from a long evening gown to a cocktail dress. The usual rule of thumb is the later the hour, the longer the dress. Also, while a small bit of 'bling' is acceptable, don't overdo it.

SEMI-FORMAL

To me, 'semi-formal' means a suit and plain tie for men; and, for women, a knee-length cocktail dress, a suit or a smart dress.

SMART CASUAL

I hate the term, I have to say, because you don't know what it means. Generally, 'no jeans' tightens things up a lot, and you'd probably wear a jacket but no tie. For men, 'smart casual' also means a shirt with a collar. For women, interestingly, Emily Post permits the wearing of jeans but stipulates that they have to be smart! This is probably because men's jeans tend to be messy, baggy affairs, and women's are generally tidier and can be dressed up more readily. Again, this depends on the milieu: a lawyer friend of mine knows that jeans would be completely unacceptable even at a casual out-of-office lunch, so she has to settle for a skirt and blouse (no jacket) or a semi-casual dress instead.

CASUAL

Some offices now have 'dress-down Fridays', and it can be difficult to know the meaning of 'casual wear', particularly in an office setting. For men, the options are generally for a pair of slacks rather than jeans, a polo shirt or a plain T-shirt with no logos on it, and a jacket of some kind. For women, smart jeans and a blouse, rather than a T-shirt, might work; but, again, this depends on your environment. In some offices there's an unspoken 'no denim' rule, so, if you're new, gauge what your colleagues are wearing before you jump in. You're not expected to turn up in your tracksuit, and shorts and flip-flops would also be an absolute no-no. When it comes to trainers, it depends on your industry: if it's a formal one, trainers wouldn't work, even on 'casual' days.

RESORT DRESS

This is a new category, reflecting the amount of travel people do nowadays. According to *Vogue*, 'The term "cruise" or "resort" came from its origins as a collection from which designers' jet-set clients purchased pieces for their (northern hemisphere) summer holidays, such as resorts or cruises. Although overseas travel has become more prevalent and the rise of tools such as worldwide internet shopping has made this less relevant, the pre-collections have become an important event on many designers' calendars.' Now you know! Of course, if you're in the Breakers in Florida, resort dress might mean a jacket and open-necked shirt. If you're on a skiing holiday in the Rockies, you'll be needing a nice warm parka and boots.

The patent-leather shoes

We don't wear dress shoes in Ireland, as a rule, but they're very popular in America and are often worn as part of a police uniform, believe it or not. They're patent leather, which reminds me of a great story a friend of mine told me about patent-leather shoes.

He was in Florida on holiday and was late for his return flight to Ireland. Rushing to the airport with his wife and kids, he was stopped by a policeman for speeding. The policeman was so upset about the speed my friend was doing that he demanded he follow him to the station.

When my friend got there, accompanied by his seven-year-old son, the policeman led him into the station, where there were two other policemen sitting at a table. The first one proceeded to march up and down, asking the other two, 'Can you guess what speed this man was doing, with children in the car?'

One policeman guessed 55 miles an hour; the other said 70.

But the deputy shook his head, steadily becoming more and more enraged. 'I'll tell you what this man was doing: 105 miles an hour, with children in the car.'

At this stage he was nose to nose with my friend, but as the deputy was roaring at him, my friend's child kept tugging at his trousers. 'Daddy, I'm going to…'

The next thing, the child threw up all over the policeman, spattering his trousers and his lovely patent-leather shoes. These shoes will accept that very nicely, as my friend discovered! He was fined $200 and missed the flight. And the moral of the story is… never wear dress shoes.

FUNERALS

Funerals, of course, are always sad occasions and are often ones of great emotion. The family will be under stress, or the death of the individual may have been sudden, in which case they will still be in a state of shock. It's wise to remember all these things when attending a funeral, whether of a close family member or of the relative of a friend.

Also, families can, at times, have long-running disputes, and these have a tendency to surface at formal events such as funerals. I've heard loud conversations about wills and who would inherit at one funeral, which is clearly inappropriate. If the funeral is of a close family member I generally try to think that, for the sake of yourself and your siblings, you should put your problems aside for the day and get on with the event, before going back to the problem. If your father or mother dies and you haven't spoken to your brothers and sisters for some time, they'll go to the funeral, and you'll be the one who loses out, with all the guilty feelings that go with it. I honestly feel that, in life, there are times when you have to put your own feelings to one side and focus on the deceased and what they would have wanted.

If you're a friend of someone whose mother or father has died, I think it's a lovely idea to go to the funeral. Your friend won't think you're being invasive or nosy: they will value your support. If you're bereaved you'll always remember who came to your mother's or father's funeral.

BEING APPROPRIATE

For immediate family, dressing for a funeral is generally straightforward: black or dark colours are the norm and, for a man, a dark suit and tie. In Ireland until quite recently the general congregation didn't wear black for a funeral, but rather their Sunday best. Clearly, no loud colours or fancy prints is a good rule.

The other thing to remember at funerals is warmth: I have a 'funeral coat', a warm, dark coat I always wear to funerals because I'll be standing outside the church for half an hour. And bring an umbrella in case you get caught in a shower at the graveside.

Of course, funerals take many forms nowadays, but at a service, no matter what the denomination, it's best to be quiet and reflective and to keep any loud chatter for outside. If you have a cold and need to blow your nose loudly, or if you need to quieten your noisy toddler, pop down the back of the church to do so.

Make sure you arrive on time for the service, but if you're late be discreet about making your entrance—no crashing up the centre of the church while the prayers are in full swing. Find the seat closest to the back and sit down quietly. If you'd like to move forward later, you can.

Of course, it goes without saying that at funerals good behaviour is a must. So be careful to moderate your alcohol intake at any funeral lunch and to observe protocols on seating. Remember to offer your condolences to the close family afterwards. It can be difficult to think of the right words, but often a simple hug or handshake will be perfect. You want the family to know that you're there and that you care. And don't forget to sign the book of condolences; the family may have missed you and they can sit down afterwards and look at the book and remember your words.

If you're a close family member of someone who has died, funerals can be daunting. It seems that there are a number of hurdles to cross, and these can seem overwhelming, particularly at a time of grief. However, most religious funerals do have a fairly strict format, and you'll be guided through this by the director of the funeral home and by the person who'll be officiating at the ceremony.

If the funeral is a secular one, there won't be that structure to rely on and so you'll probably need to think about creating a suitable format yourself. But the venue, for example the crematorium, will guide you on this. Common to all funerals is, of course, the eulogy, if one is allowed. Always check with the funeral celebrant whether a eulogy is permitted.

THE EULOGY

If you'll be performing a eulogy, perhaps try to think of it as an opportunity to say what you'd like to say about the deceased. The congregation will absolutely be on your side and supportive, so don't worry about making mistakes. You don't need to sum up their life story in every minute detail: just give a sense of who they were as a person, or even recall an incident in their life that conveys the kind of person they were. Many people will enjoy hearing you talk about their dad's passion for golf or their mother's for gardening, or about memories of happy family holidays and Christmases.

If the deceased had problems, I think it's best to be honest about them and not to try to pretend they didn't exist; otherwise it really will be the elephant in the room, so to speak. You don't need to be specific or to regale the congregation with unpleasant incidents: just acknowledge that there were struggles or difficulties and move on.

The key with eulogies, I think, is to be personal. At a time when funerals are no longer always conducted by the family priest, who would have known the deceased well, it's all the more important that someone talks about them in a personal way. And gentle humour is just fine. I came across this very nice anecdote on the website www.rip.ie:

At the memorial service for comedian Ronnie Barker in London's Westminster Cathedral the cross was accompanied

up the aisle by four candles (or fork 'andles, if you prefer), a
reference to a famous sketch in one of his shows.

In his eulogy, comedian Ronnie Corbett told the story of when
Barker first went into a private hospital in North London for
tests on his ailing heart and told the porter pushing his
wheelchair that he didn't want anyone to know he was there.
'Oh, we're very, very discreet in here,' the porter assured him.
'In fact, we had Danny La Rue in on Thursday.'

You might also find that you'd like to include a quote or
two about death in your eulogy. There are many suitable ones
to be found, from Gandhi to Ecclesiastes to Ralph Waldo
Emerson. Here's an example from Thomas Grey of the kind
of thing I mean:

If I should die and leave you
Be not like the others, quick undone
Who keep long vigils by the silent
dust and weep.

For my sake turn to life and smile
Nerving thy heart and trembling
hand to comfort weaker souls than thee.
Complete these unfinished tasks of mine
And I perchance may therein comfort thee.

SURVIVING FAMILY OCCASIONS

No matter how well we might get on with our families, there's nothing like a family occasion—whether it's a birthday, Christmas or a silver wedding anniversary—to magnify any family difficulties. We're grown up and have gone about our daily lives and may even have families of our own, and yet the minute we step over the threshold of our family home we start squabbling with our brothers and sisters, and resenting Mum for asking us to do the washing up… or worse. Many of us would like to experience the 'perfect family occasion', but it's not always possible, even in the happiest of families.

I think it's important to remember one thing: you don't have to revert to your ten-year-old self with your family. You're now an adult and can choose to behave like one, no matter what the provocation. Maybe your sister starts teasing you about how untidy, forgetful or scattered you were when you were twelve—just rise above it and bring the conversation around to what you're doing now. You don't have to bite back by recalling some embarrassing incident from your childhood; instead, talk about your holiday to Brazil or the volunteering work you're doing. The same goes for the role you play in your family. Maybe they expect you to host Christmas for them all, because you've always been the organiser. Well, you can simply say that you have other plans or are going to Paris this year! Once Mum and

Dad are too elderly to host Christmas the children should take it in turns.

If you have stressful family relationships, can you try to put them to one side, just for one day? This may seem like the most difficult thing in the world, but try to remember that it really is only one day, and then you can return to your life. The same goes for the unpopular guest——Auntie Bridie, say, who always complains that the turkey is undercooked and that she hasn't got enough roast potatoes. You'll have to grit your teeth, but, try not to get upset. Auntie Bridie is probably secretly delighted that someone wants her for Christmas. It can really help too if you set limits on her visit. Offer to drop her home after dinner so that you can control how long she stays. In fact, setting limits on your own stay might well help you to survive it, if you're finding it difficult. Go for a couple of hours and then say that you have a drinks party to go to…

Mums and dads set great store by Christmas, as a rule, and hate to have it spoiled by bickering, so if you can think about keeping them happy it might help. A friend of mine has been separated from her husband for a number of years, but she continued to visit her mother-in-law with her son and ex-husband until her mother-in-law's death in her eighties. My friend did this because she liked her and didn't want to upset her, and she felt that she could give up one hour of her Christmas Day to visit her with her family. Everyone was happy.

The other thing to bear in mind is that Christmas, especially, is really all about the children. To me, Christmas morning is very important for young families, and children should open their presents then. Making them wait until the afternoon is torture… There's something very special about Christmas morning, when the house is in bedlam and we're all looking at our new things.

Alcohol also looms large at many an Irish celebration. Remember, whether it's a wedding, Christmas or Holy Communion, it's a long day, so it pays not to overdo it and then feel worse for wear in the middle of the afternoon—or, indeed, to decide that it's time to deliver some home truths!

And be realistic about your expectations for any family event. You won't suddenly turn into the Waltons because you've been thrown together for a day to celebrate a nephew's Confirmation. Be realistic and practical about what you can do to negotiate the day and even to enjoy it. As the comedian George Burns said, 'Happiness is having a large, loving, caring, close-knit family in another city.'

Planes, trains and automobiles

'I travel not to go anywhere, but to go. I travel for travel's sake.
The great affair is to move.'
—Robert Louis Stevenson

I TRAVEL an awful lot, and I can honestly say I've experienced most of the world's travel systems, so I like to think I'm a bit of an expert. I've taken taxis in New York, where it's practically an Olympic event, and flown on most major airlines, and I also have to drive a lot when we're filming 'At Your Service', so transport is my speciality! I think that transport is the thing that's changed most since the early days. Certainly air travel used to be a high-class affair, full of glamour and expense, and now it could hardly be more different. With everyone squashed into tiny spaces nowadays, behaving well has become more and more important.

DRIVING

A friend of mine was in his car at the traffic lights in Galway when an elderly American couple pressed the button to use the pedestrian crossing. Through his open window he could hear the exchange as the lights turned green for pedestrians, accompanied by that *beep beep* for the visually impaired. The man began to cross, but his wife didn't know what the sound was and hesitated by the lights, so he walked back to her and said, 'It's okay, honey, you can cross now.'

'What's that noise?' she asked.

'Oh, it's for the blind people,' he replied helpfully, leading her across the crossing.

'They let blind people drive in Ireland?' she was heard to say as she crossed.

We don't let partially sighted people drive in Ireland, but we do have a number of rules, both official and unspoken, when it comes to driving. They are there for a reason: to make driving more pleasant for everyone and, more importantly, to make it safer. I think we Irish drivers would agree that safety has been a big concern in recent years, and quite rightly so. Cutting other people up, overtaking on bends, tailgating, flashing lights and constantly using the horn are all not only rude but also dangerous. I have to say, I've used the horn in my car only three times in twenty years, and then really just to say hello to someone I know. Yes, I know... I shouldn't use the horn for this purpose, but, in my defence, it was in the countryside!

I think people can get a bit aggressive in their cars, because they forget where they are. So many of us now live in the car, with long journeys to work and suchlike, that we can get lost in our own little world and forget that there are other people on the road. And driving can turn the most mild-mannered of people into lunatics sometimes! Here are the most important things I try to remember when I'm driving:

- Only use the horn in an emergency.

- When someone ahead of you indicates to get into your lane, let them in. You've nothing to gain by not doing so, and you'd hope someone would do the same for you.

- Remember the rules of the road on roundabouts. Americans don't have them—'rotaries', they call them, and they strike the fear of God into them! (It's not surprising if you've tried some of the bigger roundabouts in our towns and cities.) There are certain rules about taking roundabouts, which we learn for our driving test, but we're inclined to forget them. To remind you, the Road Safety Authority talks about the 'golden rule' of taking a roundabout: 'Think of the roundabout as a clock. If taking any exit from the six o'clock to the twelve o'clock position, motorists should generally approach in the left-hand lane. If taking any exit between the twelve o'clock and the six o'clock positions, motorists should generally approach in the right-hand lane.' Now you know.

- Follow the road signs: they are there for a reason. Don't ignore stop signs, yield signs or one-way street signs in particular.

- Don't drive too close to the car in front: it's dangerous. If that car is slow and you want to overtake, don't do so on a bend or where there's a continuous white line. Needless to say, look out for oncoming cars: there's nothing more frightening than seeing an overtaking car barrelling towards you as you drive!

- Don't race through pedestrian crossings at the last minute—you never know, someone might be trying to cross. If you can see that the light is turning orange, slow down and wait.

- There are many more cyclists on our roads than there used to be, so be aware of them. Give them plenty of space and always check in your wing mirror and your blind spot if you're turning left.

- Speeding is dangerous. According to the Road Safety Authority, it was a factor in 22 per cent of fatalities between 1997 and 2011. Many of these occurred in 80 and 100 km/h zones. In Europe, speeding is a factor in eleven thousand deaths every year, which makes for alarming reading. Furthermore, one in ten people will die in an accident at 30 km/h, and this increases to nine in ten at 60 km/h. So, slowing down isn't just about being polite: it's about saving lives.

• Don't use your mobile phone in the car. I know it's hard not to, because when you're sitting there driving and the phone goes off it's almost an instinct to want to answer it. But don't—it's dangerous. I've lost count of the number of people I see driving and texting or calling, and I can't think that they would be driving safely. How many of us have seen someone not indicating and taking a corner wide because they're on the phone? And if you don't believe me, the RSA tells us that using your mobile makes you four times more likely to crash... You have been warned! If you're likely to be distracted by your phone, switch it to silent or put it in the glove compartment, where you can't reach it. If you're waiting for a phone call or message just pull over to check your phone every so often.

If you use taxis at all you'll have a taxi story: there's something about being in a confined space with a stranger, often in an unfamiliar place... As far as I'm concerned, New York is by far the most difficult city to hail a taxi in. There's none of this civilised Hailo business, where a taxi finds you by means of an app on your smartphone. No, in New York it's dog eat dog!

If I stand on the corner and hail a taxi, but someone else runs up beside me and puts one foot in front of me, the taxi will stop for them. Whoever is nearest the door wins the taxi battle—it's that competitive. In Dublin or in other places in Ireland, getting a taxi is positively sedate by comparison.

Sometimes a taxi journey can be a truly hair-raising experience. I still shiver when I think of one I took in Buenos Aires in a thunderstorm. Four of us had left the Alvear Palace Hotel to go to the airport, and we sped down the motorway at 110 miles an hour—in a beat-up Renault, in the lashing rain, with lightning and thunder crashing around us. Sure why not! I was terrified: the car was aquaplaning all over the place, with lorries and cars thundering past. As if that wasn't bad enough, after about twenty minutes we began to slow down, eventually stopping in the middle of the motorway! The car just ground to a halt. I thought, 'In the name of God, are we out of petrol?' I couldn't believe it—running out of petrol on the motorway. The driver began to turn the key in the engine, but there was no response. So he turned the key again, and, the next thing, the engine started. By this stage I was in a cold sweat, and I hardly dared wonder what had gone on. Then the driver waved his hand back and forth and repeated, 'Petrol, gas. Petrol, gas.' I remembered seeing a gas tank in the boot; he'd run out of petrol and needed to switch the engine over to gas—in the middle of the fast lane. We took off again, but I didn't dare breathe until we got to the airport.

Hopefully you won't have any such taxi journeys from hell, but a few pointers will help make your journey more pleasant:

1. Firstly, we have a lovely habit in this country of getting into the taxi beside the driver. I suppose it's more friendly,

but the car is the workplace of the driver, and, as far as I'm concerned, if I were a taxi-driver I wouldn't want someone sitting on top of me in my office. So, I prefer to sit behind the driver. Besides, there's a bit of an unwritten rule that if there's a crowd of you getting into a taxi the person who sits beside the driver pays, so that's another good reason to sit behind. I always get stuck like that!

2. If you don't want to talk to the driver, you don't have to. Simply say, 'Good morning. O'Connell Street, please. I'm doing a little work here.' Or I take out a book and read it. I let him know what I'll be doing in the car. You don't need to bite their head off: just politely indicate that you're busy.

3. The driver will generally presume you don't know the route, so they may not necessarily take the most direct one to your destination. You can just say nicely, 'Would you mind taking the Jack Lynch Tunnel?' or whatever. If you don't know the area, you're at the mercy of the driver. I got into a tiff one night with a taxi-driver in New York years ago. He took off at fifty or sixty miles an hour up Manhattan, all because he didn't fancy driving me to Queens, since he would have struggled to get a fare back. So he just deposited me on 125th Street—which was not the trendy place it is now, I can tell you. He was very aggressive, and I could have got into a row with him, but I decided not to. It pays to re-member that the driver is in control, in order to avoid altercations. But it's also the driver's job to make you com-fortable on your journey, so if you want them to roll the window down or lower the volume on the radio, you're quite entitled to ask. And let's not forget, many taxi-drivers are friendly, courteous and helpful, so hopefully you won't need to be giving out about them!

4. If you have a minor complaint—if the driver is rude or their car isn't clean—you can say it, nicely, but weigh up the benefits of doing so. You might simply decide to exit the taxi, having paid no tip, and put it down to experience. If, however, you do need to make a complaint—about overcharging, say—make sure you take down the driver's licence number before you leave the car. The Transport for Ireland website (www.transportforireland.ie) contains an online form for feedback, on which you can raise your complaint. You can also officially compliment the driver using the same form, which might be nice if they've been very helpful.

5. I always tip taxi-drivers. If the fare is small, say €6.50, I'd round it up and add one euro, to €7.50 or so. If it's €8.80 I'd make it €10. If it's a long fare I'd normally tip at 15 per cent. You don't have to, but I think taxi-drivers have to put up with a lot, and a little bit of appreciation goes a long way.

The 'Noddy' bus

I don't often take the bus, because I live in the countryside, but I have fond memories of one 'bus' journey in particular. It was 1985, and the RAC—that's the Royal Automobile Club—decided that they were going to publish a guide to Ireland, because they hadn't done so in a number of years. To launch it they invited a group of hoteliers to London for a big function. They put us up in the Stafford Hotel, which was a lovely place, and invited us to a black-tie dinner. When we came down to reception they'd hired a vintage 1935 British Leyland bus to take us to the clubhouse—a shiny silver-and-green one which reminded me of something from Noddy! In we all got and went *put-put-put* down the glorious Pall Mall, with all those big white buildings, to the RAC clubhouse.

Afterwards everyone was a bit tipsy—except for me, of course—and we rolled out into the freezing November night, climbing back on the bus again. The driver turned the key in the ignition and… nothing, apart from a brief rattle of the engine.

I went up to him and asked, 'Would a push work?' He replied that that would be brilliant, but he looked doubtfully at the crowd in their monkey suits. 'Not a bother,' I said, 'Off the bus, boys, we have to push.' So there we were, pushing the Noddy bus for the RAC up the Mall! We got it started, and off we rolled home, delighted with ourselves.

PUBLIC TRANSPORT

Buses have moved on a bit since 1935, but, as in anything in life, if there are other people involved you have to try your best to be considerate.

According to the website www.uncommon-courtesy.com, in Russia, where the trains and buses are very crowded, if you step on someone's foot accidentally, they will quite happily step back on yours—hard! Also, the trains are often so crowded there that people are lifted off their feet. I suppose it makes a change from Tokyo, where they use huge paddles, like oars, to press passengers into the carriages. (According to the same website, in Bangkok everything stops for the national anthem. Passengers stop dead on the platform for the duration of the anthem, before continuing on their way.)

One thing Russian passengers also do, though, according to the researcher, is get up when an elderly person gets on the bus. Sadly, we can't say the same thing in Ireland, where many people look vacantly out the window when they see an elderly person looking for a seat. There's no question but that you should give an older, or infirm, person your seat. It's a 'no-brainer', as far as I'm concerned. The same goes for pregnant women and, indeed, women with small children.

The other thing to remember when getting on the bus or train is to **let the other passengers off first**. I have to confess that sometimes I have got on first, but only because the passenger was hesitating and the doors were about to close. Use your discretion, but remember: you can't really get on until the passengers have got off—at least not without a struggle. When you're on the bus don't block the passageway if it's very busy: move to the back. And if you're getting off at the next stop, let other people pass you while you stay where you are. Finally, try not to wait until the last possible moment to leave the bus or train. Instead, gather your belongings and be ready to get off.

Don't put your feet on the seats. It's not just that it's rude: you're preventing another passenger from sitting down. I remember a good story from a friend of mine about this. She was travelling in Morocco on a busy train, in one of those compartments that seat six passengers or so, when a big, burly soldier got on and promptly put his feet up on the seats. No-one had the nerve to challenge him, and so they all just waited. My friend had to climb over his legs to go out to the toilet! Next thing, he pulls a little pink facecloth from his pocket and drapes it over his shoulder. 'What on earth could he be doing?' wondered my friend. She soon found out: he proceeded to nod off, feet still up on the opposite seat, and to dribble all over the facecloth! He woke up refreshed after his catnap, folded up the towel, wiped his face with it and put it away.

Silence, or the lack of it, is one of the big complaints on buses and trains nowadays. Many train companies now have 'silent carriages' so that passengers can escape the noise of mobile phones, iPods and laptops, but if you're travelling on a bus or train and are using an electronic device, be considerate. Dutch people have told me that they shout into their phones by force of habit, as the phone lines were so bad in the 1940s and 1950s, but today there's no excuse. So don't use your mobile on loudspeaker—a baffling thing I've seen a few times recently—and turn down the volume on your laptop if you're watching YouTube. Better still, plug in a pair of earphones and make sure there's no noise leaking from them. Also, if you're chatting to a friend on your mobile, that's just fine, but try not to shout or laugh hysterically: not everyone wants to hear your account of your stressful day at the office or your 'best jokes' of the day.

Eating on public transport is one of those things that can really annoy others—but it depends. In many countries it's considered perfectly acceptable. In Japan they even have a word for it: *ekiben* ('train lunch box'), a specially made and delicious-looking mixture of sushi and tempura. I'm personally not a fan of eating when out and about like this, because I think much of our fast food here can be pretty smelly and unappetising. A burger or bag of curried chips probably isn't the thing! The same goes for drinking anything other than water, or tea or coffee in a takeaway cup. I remember a time when drinking beer on the Tube in London was considered perfectly acceptable. It was banned only in 2008. The simple rule of thumb, as far as I'm concerned, is that public transport is not an extension of your home, so try to remember that. One piece of advice that stood out when I was researching this book was for parents not to change nappies on the Underground—the very idea!

PLANES

Never are manners so important as when you're travelling on an aircraft. Modern air travel has us all packed in like sardines, and that's after having had to remove what feels like every stitch of clothing in security. It's vital that we remember our manners, both before and during the flight. This can be difficult for us all, particularly those travelling with children or elderly people, when the whole experience seems to be extremely stressful. But we try! I think there are five steps to comfortable air travel.

1. BEFORE YOU LEAVE

I travel an awful lot, so I've fine-tuned the art of packing, because I haven't got time to carry heavy suitcases: I need to zip on and off the flight. Many travellers nowadays also want to avoid paying fees for excess baggage and so will be filling only one of those small wheelie suitcases. Here are my tips for packing that little suitcase.

- Check your airline's baggage restrictions before you pack, and measure your suitcase to make sure it meets the criteria. I know that this might sound a bit extreme, but you'll thank me when the airline representative approaches you with the measuring tape!

- Wear your heaviest shoes, and only pack a light pair in your suitcase. Shoes are very heavy, so try to restrict yourself to the minimum number of pairs to get by. If you're going to a sunny place don't bring your boots: pack something for walking and something for the beach.

- Make sure your toiletries are no more than 100 ml in size and pack them in a clear plastic bag. Many chemists now do little travel packs in a clear toilet bag.

- When it comes to clothes, many of us pack the kitchen sink in order to prepare for every eventuality. But because you have a limited amount of space it pays to think carefully about what you'll need.

  If it will be chilly you might need your winter coat, in which case wear it or sling it over your arm. But will you also need that woolly jumper or jacket? If you do, can you get away with lightweight versions, or with layers that can be taken off if it gets too warm?

  If it's going to be sunny you can fold lightweight, packable dresses or slacks and one jacket into your case. Why not check the weather forecast before you go, just to be sure.

  When you're packing try to stick to neutral colours—not for fashion reasons, but because from a practical standpoint they're easier to mix and match. Try to remember any special events you'll need to pack for—that black-tie dinner or the beach barbecue you'll need a swimming suit for.

- When packing, start with the bigger items and then pack the other things around them. I find that rolling items, rather than folding them, helps me keep things relatively free from creases, and I can fit more into my suitcase. I also find that wrapping clothes in tissue paper can help if you want to avoid creasing.

- Don't be tempted to pack your case to the rafters, as you'll only end up exceeding the baggage restrictions—and you won't have any room for souvenirs!

- A good tip when packing is to put your fragile things in the middle of the case, where they're less likely to be damaged. My top tip is to pack underwear and socks into your shoes, where there's all that empty space. The trick is to make the maximum use of a small space.

Before you head to the airport, check in online and make sure that you have the correct ID. Finally, double-check your suitcase to make sure you don't have any bottles or toiletries over 100 ml.

2. AT THE AIRPORT

As we all know, many airports are more or less in complete chaos nowadays, with people rushing all over the place and with long queues for security. Maybe it's because I travel a lot, but I have to say that it never ceases to amaze me how many people don't get ready for security in advance, in spite of the long wait. Instead, they look a bit bewildered when they get to the security area and only then start to get ready. I always have comfortable clothes to travel in, because I need to bear in mind that I'll have to disrobe when I get to the airport. And remember, upgrades tend to be given to the better-dressed person, so you might not want to follow the example of the Arizona businessman who dresses in women's underwear and heels for every flight!

While I'm waiting in line I undo my shoelaces, loosen my belt, take off my jacket and make sure that all my toiletries are in the clear plastic bag. No bottles of water or tubes of toothpaste in your suitcase! Most importantly, I remember to take my laptop out of my suitcase. Then, when it comes to my turn, I just have to pop my things into the tray and slide it along the conveyor belt through the scanner. When the tray comes out the other end I try to take my things promptly and put the tray aside for the next person.

I'm sure you all know this by now, but there are certain things that are prohibited by security. Check these before you bring that side of ham or that big jar of jam with you. And no pen-knives or anything like that. (That includes larger nail scissors, by the way, so you might want to leave the manicure set at home.) Also, if you have a nice bottle of expensive perfume or aftershave, remember that it should be no more than 100 ml or it may well be confiscated. A friend of mine was stopped recently in possession of a set of Allen keys for his bicycle!

3. Boarding the plane

Once you've cleared security the next hurdle is boarding the plane. Many airlines are now moving away from the practice of not allocating seating, so hopefully this won't be the free-for-all it once was. A few simple rules will keep you sane.

- Once you've found your seat, try not to take all day to take your coat off, put your case in the overhead locker and put your newspaper on the seat. I always politely say, 'Could

you step in, because there's a queue behind me,' if somebody is dithering in finding their seat. Put your wheelie
case in with its wheels facing in towards the wall: it's a
rounded area, so the case will fit in much better. If you put
the wheels out towards the aisle, the locker door won't
close, and it will accommodate only two bags, not three.
Also, don't worry too much about your coat: if you sit
down and wait the steward will put your coat up for you,
on top of the suitcases in the overhead locker, because they
know the drill.

- If you have any walking difficulties or are elderly, ask if you
can sit at the front of the plane, if seating is unallocated.
The steward will be happy to help you, so that you don't
have to struggle to the back of the plane.

- If you're sitting in an aisle seat and someone comes along
who wants to sit at the window, don't get up and block the
corridor: step over to the seats opposite, then move back
when the other person has sat down.

4 . IN FLIGHT

Once you've settled yourself down in your seat, listened to
the in-flight announcements and put your phone in flight
mode, you can relax—provided the other passengers are behaving themselves! It's harder nowadays, with everyone
squashed into a tiny space, and when I looked into the issue
for this book I was astonished at the amount of rage people
felt about the behaviour of passengers on flights. In a CNN

survey of the most irritating behaviour, respondents got hot under the collar about smelly fellow passengers, legs sticking out into the aisles, and the carrying out of—ahem—'personal hygiene' activities such as flossing and the wiping of underarms with wet wipes (God help us). Top of the list, though, was kicking or pushing the seat in front of you. Other pet peeves included wearing heavy perfume or aftershave, smelling of onions (!) and taking off shoes. It was a real eye-opener for me, I can tell you!

Some people get very annoyed about other people's chatter on flights. As far as I'm concerned, to talk or not to talk is one of the big in-flight questions. It's something you either like or you don't. I've had some fascinating conversations on flights. Once, on a flight to Germany, I got chatting to a lovely man who was an inventor. One of his inventions was the Mercedes single windscreen wiper. A relative of mine by marriage had invented the double wiper in 1918 for Ford, and we had a great chat about it and all his other inventions.

Another time I met a lovely country man on a long-haul flight. I'd treated myself to a business-class flight and was sitting comfortably in Row 5. Then he appeared, carrying a case with a Castletownbere sticker on it. His hands were well worn, and I wondered if he was a fisherman, but I didn't like to ask. I got the impression that he hadn't taken a flight before, because when the meal arrived he insisted he didn't want anything, until I mentioned that it was free, and he happily accepted it. I started talking to him, and it turned out that he was indeed a fisherman, and he had taken his boat all the way to Taiwan. Under some kind of maritime law he was entitled to get a business-class flight home. He was such a lovely man, and we had a great chat. I was tickled pink when it came to coffee time: he took one of those little plastic tubs of milk and popped it into the coffee like an ice cube. A memorable encounter!

Generally speaking, though, if you start a conversation it can go on for the duration of the flight, so remember that before you start! I'm always conscious that maybe I don't want to talk at all, especially on an early-morning flight, so I will have a book or magazine open on my lap. I say hello very nicely, then go back to my book. That's polite, but you're saying, I'm not here to talk. If I get caught in a lengthy conversation I have a pair of earphones at the ready, and I pick my moment to say, 'I'm going to listen to a bit of music for a while, so we'll talk later.' It generally does the trick.

If you're on a long-haul flight you'll probably need to use the toilet at some stage; but if you're on a flight from Dublin to London you might want to hold it in! It can be particularly difficult on short-haul flights to dodge the steward's trolley as it goes up the aisle, so waiting might be the best policy. However, if you're a frequent user of the bathroom, don't be afraid to either book an aisle seat or say to your fellow passenger before take-off, 'I have a little illness, and I'm going to need to use the toilet, so could I possibly have the aisle seat?' People don't mind, as a rule. If you do need to get up and have to step over your fellow passengers, who might be asleep, try to be considerate about it.

Try also to be considerate about that big bugbear for passengers, the seat-back. I was in an aisle seat on a flight once, and a big, powerful man was sitting in the window seat beside me. He went to get up and pulled at the back of the seat in front of him: the woman sitting there nearly landed in beside the pilot, she was catapulted forward so vigorously! It was straight out of *Airplane!* But it's not nice, so try to be thoughtful both when you want to rest and when you want to eat. At mealtimes I always pull my seat into the upright position, as it gives the person behind me more space.

The funny thing is, when people are on a flight they tend to behave in ways in which they wouldn't normally in public. For some reason they can forget that they're not at home while they're stuck in this tin can forty thousand feet above sea level. Mortal sins include the following:

- *Fighting over the armrests.* The battle of the pointed elbows! I think the fairest thing is to allow the person in the middle seat to have the armrests, as the person nearest the window and the person nearest the aisle can both lean to one side, while the centre person can't. If your fellow passenger asks if you can lift the armrest, be polite.

- Yes, the *air vent* can go in fifty-five different directions, but the problem is that the other passengers don't want it pointing down their neck or to be freezing all the way to New York. If you can't point it directly at yourself, just turn it off.

- Don't *lift the window blind* on a long-haul flight if it will blind your fellow passengers—and no glare from your tablet computer or mobile phone if you can possibly help it. The same goes for watching in-flight films and listening to music on your iPod: use earphones to keep the noise down. If you're watching a comedy, you don't have to guffaw all the way across the Atlantic. You're not in your own sitting room!

- **Snoring.** A friend of mine had a sinus problem and was an inveterate snorer. She was to take a long-haul flight to Hong Kong, so we had to go to a pharmacy to buy every single nasal decongestant known to man in order to prevent her keeping the whole plane awake. The trouble is, if your fellow passenger snores you can't really wake them up. Again, you're not in your own bed at home with a snoring spouse. I'm afraid you just have to put your earplugs in!

- **Taking up space.** You don't need to take up three seats with all your personal belongings. Space is at a premium, so try not to hog too much of it.

- There's something about **drinking** on planes… some people find that a small drink can make a flight bearable, but it really can bring out the worst in people. The newspapers regularly feature stories about airborne bad behaviour, and passengers are now routinely ejected from flights—not while in the air, of course!—for drunken behaviour. If you want to drink, do so in moderation, and remember that air pressure can do funny things! If you have the bad luck to be stuck beside someone who's drunk, don't engage with them: leave it to the steward.

- In a recent Lonely Planet survey, passengers on a flight were asked to rank **smells** in order of their offensiveness. Most unpleasant was feet, followed by baby vomit (!). Onions and BO also featured highly, as did stale cigarettes. Yuck.

5. DISEMBARKING

If you've survived your flight it can be tempting to throw off your seatbelt and jump up the minute the plane touches the runway, but try to resist. You'll only have to stand there for another fifteen minutes while the aircraft taxis into position. Instead, gather up your book and any electronic devices, put your jacket on and wait. Once the plane has stopped, and only then, get up and carefully open the overhead locker. Offer to help people who need it, particularly the elderly. Double check that you have everything with you, then wait in the queue to disembark. Don't try to overtake a seated passenger on the way out—you really won't gain much by it. Be a gentleman or -woman and let them get up and leave before you.

TRAVELLING ON A PLANE WITH CHILDREN

In many surveys passengers say that a crying baby or child is the most annoying aspect of their flight. There's nothing a crying baby can really do about this, and very often the air pressure is a cause of pain and discomfort. Sometimes it can be nice to simply ask if there's anything you can do to help. Parents might appreciate it if you hold the baby while they have a quick bite to eat. You're not a babysitter, but if you feel comfortable offering, why not?

However, sometimes I have to say that parents can seem to be unaware that their children's behaviour is affecting other passengers. If you're a parent and need to get on a flight with your little one, bear in mind these few helpful hints in order to make your journey, and other people's, more pleasant.

- Bring your lightest, most foldable buggy onto the plane so that it's easy to fold and stow away. Now is not the time for one of those all-terrain vehicles the same size as the aircraft! Also, ask if you can wheel the buggy right up to the departure gate, as you don't have to struggle then with bags and toys.

- Many airports have crèches for young children. Have a look online before you set out to the airport; you may find an option to buy a couple of hours of peace and quiet.

- Bring plenty of toys, games and puzzles to keep your kids busy. Also take lots of small, healthy snacks with you to distract them when boredom threatens.

- Don't let your little darling kick the back of the seat in front of them. It's really annoying for the person in that seat.

- Electronic devices can be a boon, but produce them at strategic moments or the novelty will quickly wear off.

- If your child is under two they're supposed to sit on your knee, but if the flight isn't too busy you may be able to spread out a bit. In a Mumsnet survey on travelling with children, one parent suggested that you pop your little darling down in the spare seat with a nice, smelly packet of crisps or some messy item of food. Your fellow passengers won't want to approach to ask for the seat!

- Air pressure can be an awful problem for young children, so give them something to chew on take-off. For a baby, feed them a bottle: the sucking motion will clear their ears.

You have now completed the first and second circles of life and have launched yourself out into the big, wide world, your manners hopefully intact. Bon voyage!

Next I'll look at how to behave in the place where so many of us spend so much of our time: the workplace.

The
world
of work

'Would I rather be feared or loved? Easy. Both.
I want people to be afraid of how much they love me.'
—*Michael Scott*, The Office *(US)*

I DON'T work in an office with a capital O. In fact, the hotel business is a particular kind of 'office' where you might not see your colleagues for days on end if you're working different shifts, and where you have periods when you're madly busy and others when things are much quieter. Peaks and troughs are all part of hotel life. You're also dealing with the public constantly, and this brings its own challenges. That said, when any group of people work together, a certain set of rules apply. I need to get on with all the members of staff in the hotel, just as I would if I worked in an office or shop or restaurant. Quite honestly, I've never worked anywhere where we didn't get on, because I won't tolerate it.

THE INTERVIEW

Before we even set foot in a workplace, though, we have to get that job, which means being interviewed. I have to interview people all the time for the Park, and I can't think of anything more challenging, for them or me! I tend to look for certain things in hotel staff; these may or may not apply to you, but they might give you some insight into how an employer views you.

First of all, I look for someone who has a good personality. I'm not going to be impressed with someone who's as dead as a doornail, because I work in the hospitality industry, and we need to have people with outgoing personalities.

Next, I look for a work ethic that has been there since they were young. I have to say that I set great store by a strong work ethic. Maybe it comes from my own efforts at making a few bob as a teenager, when I used to have a babysitting business, among other things. I was only about thirteen or fourteen, but the Gallaghers had built about six hundred houses at the top of our road, and I thought there had to be something all these people would want. And then I hit on it: babysitting. The place was full of young families, so it was a ready-made market. The father of my friend Brian Duffy had a factory down in Grand Canal Dock, and I ran off six hundred copies of an ad on a Gestetner machine, a forerunner of the photocopier. I dropped them in all the doors, and I had an instant business: one night I had forty-two people working for me, and I took 10 per cent. I've always had a bit of an entrepreneurial spirit!

So when I interview potential members of staff at the hotel I ask them if they did any babysitting or any work in a shop or boutique on a Saturday. Bear in mind, here, that a lot of my staff are very young, many still in their teens. I always look for potential, as you can bring personality on.

I also ask people to turn their pockets out—no, really! I just want to see if you're analytical and organised in your mind and if you know what's in your pockets. It might not seem orthodox, but it yields results. I also look at how the candidate walks away when they leave the interview. If they slope off, with slumped shoulders and their hands in their pockets, I hesitate: I like a nice, sprightly walk, full of energy.

The other thing I look for in potential employees is a sense that they will be able to think on their feet. In the hotel business, things are always going wrong, or have to be done at the last minute, and I like to know if they'll be a bit ingenious about things. I can remember plenty of occasions at the Park where ingenuity was needed, such as our first Christmas, in 1980, when I found myself up half the night making a Santa suit…

We were all set for the festivities and had a full house, and then someone said, 'What about Santa?' I'd completely forgotten: we had no Santa to appear on Christmas Day, so one of us would have to do it. Only, we had no Santa suit either, and in those days you couldn't just order one on the internet. So off I went into Cork, to Hickey's, where I bought shiny red sateen material in Santa red, and I said, 'Don't worry, I'll make it myself.' But I had no sewing skills, and, with the busy run-up to Christmas, I never quite got around to it. So, on the night of the 24th, at two o'clock in the morning, there I was, having borrowed a sewing machine, making a Santa suit—with no pattern. Working by look, I cut the front and back and even a belt, and by four o'clock in the morning I had managed to produce a Santa suit! I was delighted with myself, but fit to die with tiredness and I still had to try the suit on, in case I needed to make any final adjustments. I put my left leg in and then tried the right, only to find that I could put the suit on only with my legs crossed: I'd sewed the seam on the right to the left leg! I had to rip it out and start again… but in the end we had our Santa, and the moral of the story is: be prepared to do it yourself!

Of course, I'll freely admit that not every employer is looking for the same set of skills—the hotel business demands a particular kind of personality, I know—but if you're going for an interview, bear the following principles in mind:

1. **Do your research on the company.** Hopefully you'll have done this when you were sending in your CV, but when you're going for an interview don't offend your inter-

viewer by not knowing anything about their organisation. Instead, impress them with your enthusiasm for it and with your knowledge of what it does. There's no need to be gushing: you can just admire their business acumen.

2. **Turn up on time.** At the hotel, timekeeping is essential, because we might have a sudden rush of guests appearing for breakfast, or a tour to check out at reception, and if one or more of the staff are late it makes everything that bit more difficult. I always look for people who are good at keeping time. This may seem obvious, but it doesn't matter how much of a genius you are or how many sales contracts you've won: if you're late you've fallen at the first fence, and your interviewer might not give you another chance.

3. **Dress appropriately for your industry.** I remember a chef turning up for an interview at the hotel. It was 1982, and he was dressed in a Hawaiian shirt, open to his navel, and I can still remember that he wore an elephant tusk on a string around his neck. I can tell you, he didn't get the job! First impressions really do count. It depends on what organisation you'll be working for, of course. Any creative business will think it odd if you turn up in a suit and tie— in fact, a trendy T-shirt and jeans from an edgy label will probably impress them more. But you'll still be expected to look smart.

Some other industries will be happy with a smart-casual look for men: well-ironed slacks (not jeans), and an open-necked shirt with a jacket. And for women, a wrap dress, for example. But if you're going for an interview as a lawyer, you'll be fully expected to wear sober colours and a suit. For men a tie will be a must—and a nice, quiet one: now is not the time to debut your Angry Birds novelty tie!

As to shoes, the no-trainers rule applies. There are lots of smart casual shoes that will work; or, with a suit, a well-polished pair of brogues. For women, I'm not sure that a very high heel is appropriate for an interview—it's formal, that's true; but remember, you'll need to walk confidently across the room, not totter! I think a mid-height heel or a wedge is just perfect.

Perfume and aftershave are also to be avoided. Of course you want to be distinctive, but let your thoughts and ideas do that for you, not the strength of your scent. The same goes for women and make-up, which should be discreet, as should your jewellery. And I'm sure I don't need to mention piercings or tattoos! Anything that invites your interviewer to form a negative opinion of you is best left at home. Why let someone judge you on your appearance alone?

4. **Present yourself professionally and cordially.** You aren't the interviewer's best friend, so you won't need to be air-kissing them: a simple handshake will do. A nice, firm one too—no limp handshakes, no bone-crushers and I think no need to grasp the interviewer's elbow. You're not a politician looking for a vote! And make eye contact and smile. If you're waiting for them in their office, you don't need to jump to attention, but you do need to stand when they come in.

5. **Switch off your mobile phone.** You don't want to be distracted or to annoy your interviewer when it goes off in the middle of the interview. If it does, just switch it off as quickly as you can. Don't look at the screen to see who it is first!

Twenty questions

If I'm conducting interviews for hotel staff, I often do so with a colleague, and we try to plan ahead and divide the questions up so that we're not repeating ourselves. My queries about work ethic aside, we're also careful to avoid personal questions of any kind, because we have no need to ask them. Most interviewers are hopefully the same, not least because it's discrimination to ask inappropriate questions.

If an interviewer asks you about your age or marital status, you don't have to tell them, nor do you have to answer questions about your religion or your citizenship, or even about whether you drink or smoke. Many employers will be fully briefed on the law, so these questions shouldn't come up. If they do, simply respond, 'I'd prefer to talk about the job, if that's okay.'

Apart from that, interviewers are usually hoping to find out more about your skills, both professional and personal, so the questions will generally fall into that pattern. 'What do you think you could bring to the job that another candidate couldn't?' 'What are your strengths and weaknesses?' That kind of thing. Many people get flummoxed when they're asked about their strengths and weaknesses, but the interviewer isn't looking for character flaws: there's no need to mention that you can't get out of bed before midday! I think you can generally turn it into a positive: 'I tend to be very enthusiastic when I work on a project and to put a lot into it.' And just in case the interviewer asks you what you find interesting about their company, have three important things already noted down that you admire and that will also show that you've done your research. I really like it when potential staff members remark on things we've done at the hotel, because it shows that they're interested.

And remember, if you're an interviewee you're also finding out if you like the employer, so don't be afraid to ask questions. But keep them to a few simple ones; you're not there to grill them. Keep your questions to the details of the job: what exactly will be involved, what your responsibilities will be—that kind of thing.

The interviewer might also ask you that old favourite, 'Where do you see yourself in five years' time?' As far as I'm concerned, the answer is not 'In your office,' nor is it the opposite: 'On a beach in Marbella'! I think the trick is to be specific and to show that you have definite goals in mind. 'I'd really like to have developed X product in foreign markets and to have finished my MBA.'

NEGOTIATING OFFICE POLITICS

When I think of 'office politics' I think of people stabbing each other in the back and playing mind games, not of them getting on with the job or actually even enjoying themselves. As far as I'm concerned, there's a right way and a wrong way to behave in working life.

1.

Be courteous, get to know your colleagues, be prepared to share a laugh (but no lewd jokes), and take an interest in how the company works.

2.

If you're a newcomer don't be afraid to ask questions: people are happy to help and, in fact, would rather do so than have you make mistakes that could have been avoided.

3.

Listen, rather than talk, at first, even if you're a chatterbox or are only dying to show what you can do. Watch how the office works and how people interact: you have to fit in with them, not the other way around.

4.

Don't get drawn into silly gossip: it's unhelpful, and if your manager is aware of negative sniping you could find yourself tarred with the same brush. It's always best to rise above it. However, it's useful to be aware of tensions and difficulties. Knowing why Mary in accounts doesn't get on with Jim in publicity can be helpful, but this doesn't mean you have to get sucked into rows.

5.

Always treat people respectfully, no matter what their status. Not only is it the right thing to do, but you never know when you might need the postman's help, for example, when you have an urgent mailing. And if you're unpleasant, word will quickly get around the office. I believe there are certain people with whom extra charm might work a treat. Always, but *always*, be nice to the boss's assistant: they're the guardian at the gate, and they control access to the person you wish to speak to. If you're nice you'll really have made a powerful ally. Also, remember that if they don't like you they won't have nice things to say about you to the boss! Never make the mistake of being rude or dismissive, as it will come back to bite you.

6.

'Never complain, and never explain' is a motto I just love. Nobody likes excuses or lengthy explanations for why things went wrong. I know *I* don't, because I honestly haven't got the time for it: I just want things to be put right! If you're late meeting a deadline on a report, a brief 'Apologies for the delay, but here's my report...' will do just fine. No need to add 'because the cat got sick on my first report and then my child scribbled all over it,' and definitely not 'Sorry my report is late; I wasn't given enough time to do it.' That sounds like an accusation, and it won't be terribly popular.

DISPLAYING EMOTION

I personally don't see anything wrong with a display of normal emotion in the office. At the Park there's plenty of emotion from time to time, because the hotel business is a stressful one and sometimes tempers get a bit frayed. I do the training sessions for the hotel staff every spring, just before the start of Easter Week, when the hotel reopens after the winter. The induction session normally takes two days, and I always say to them, 'Two of you will be in my office at the end of the week bawling crying.' I'm not trying to be mean— just impressing upon them that the hotel opening can be a baptism of fire. And, sure enough, by the end of every training week, it happens! It doesn't faze me at all, because it's entirely understandable. We aren't robots, after all, but human beings.

However, there are two things to bear in mind: there's a time and a place, and it depends on the emotion! The AGM isn't the place to display your rage at not getting a pay rise. Nor is it useful to raise the subject when you're meeting work colleagues at a drinks party, as they might just assume you're a whinger. If you have a grievance, think carefully about where you want to express it—and then how. I have plenty of people coming up to my office, but they don't storm into it yelling, 'I need to talk to you now!' It won't get them anywhere at all.

Also, I'm sure we all agree that it's not a good idea to take stress out on our fellow workers, hurling staplers or yelling, slamming doors or swearing. I don't need to tell you that physically accosting anyone is a sackable offence, but express-ing your anger appropriately is a different matter. I think it's fine to say something like 'Look, I'm a bit angry about that missed phone call, because...' or 'I need to discuss my per-formance review with you, because I'm disappointed not to have been considered for a bonus.'

Of course, there will be times when you're not at your best; when you're overwhelmed by emotion. If you can, take a moment. Don't take action straightaway, even though it may be hard not to. Just pause for a second. If you need to, take a breather and go outside for some fresh air. Come back in when you're calm and ready to deal with the situation. If you've lost your cool, for whatever reason, apologise promptly and move on.

The flambé story

On a more light-hearted note, one of my favourite 'emotion' stories is the flambé story. Remember flambés? They used to be a very popular dessert at the Park, and when you're a waiter or waitress you're always dying to do one, because it's a bit special. We used to do a fruit flambé, with white wine, brandy and fresh fruit. It works like this: you take your copper pan and warm it up, then add sugar and butter and melt it down. You then add fresh fruit, followed by the white wine, and, last of all, a drop of brandy floated across the top of the pan. Then you tip it into the flames and, hey presto! up it puffs just lightly. Delicious.

One night in the restaurant, Table 1 ordered it, and Bernie, one of the waitresses, begged to be allowed to do it. Gerry Brown, the head waiter at the time, said, 'Now, Bernie, go down there and do it right, or you lose your job.' I know, a bit drastic, but we were under pressure!

So off Bernie went with her trolley, and she was talking away to the couple while she made up the dessert. Bernie wasn't paying attention and put the sugar and butter in, then the fruit, but instead of white wine she put in a big dollop of brandy, and it went *bang, wallop!* and a huge jet of flame shot up and hit the ceiling. The word in the kitchen was that Mr Brennan had to get the ceiling painted, because Bernie had burned a hole in it! Gerry Brown came charging down and distracted the guests, rescuing the situation, and they were served their dessert, none the wiser about the near burning down of the restaurant. Gerry nearly had a stroke.

Of course, the next thing, Table 10 ordered the flambé, and Gerry pulled Bernie into the kitchen and said, 'Bernie, listen to me. Go down to Table 10, do that dessert and make no mistakes, and if you do you'll lose your job. You're under starter's orders.'

So down she went to Table 10 to put the butter and sugar on the pan and caramelise it, before adding the fruit and white wine and, finally, the little drop of brandy. It all went *puff* nice and gently, and she served it to the couple at the table.

The woman, who spoke very little English, started shaking her head. 'No, no.'

Oh, Bernie thought, maybe she doesn't want it, and so she offered it to the man, who also shook his head, 'No, no.'

'Oh, sorry,' Bernie said, mystified.

She was about to ask him if he wanted something else when he pointed to Table 1 and said, 'We want the same as that table.' They'd been so impressed at the fireworks that they wanted the same!

DEALING WITH DIFFICULT PERSONALITIES

No office is perfect. You'll always have to deal with difficult people, whether it's the office bully, the whiner or the competitive underminer of your work. Whether it's the office setting or the people themselves, they do tend to take on certain roles in the workplace. I suppose it's all down to group dynamics! Here are a few tips for dealing with difficult people:

- Have a think about the other person's actions as objectively as you can. Once you take your emotions out of it—your frustration and upset—what can you see going on, in your view?

- Try not to take things personally: your colleague's refusal to take phone calls or answer e-mails may not be directed at you. It may simply be that they have their own issues. Taking the personal sting out of their behaviour might help you to look at it in a different way.

- Of course, it can happen that a colleague takes a dislike to you, for reasons you can't fathom. If this is the case—and, of course, it's not acceptable behaviour—you need to tackle it calmly. Some experts recommend using 'I' rather than 'you' phrases. So, 'I'd really like it if you included me in that memo the next time,' instead of 'You didn't include me in that memo, and I'm really annoyed about it.'

- If you need to raise something with your difficult colleague, stick to specifics and keep it to the work. Don't make any kind of personal remarks, no matter how tempting, because things have a habit of getting overheated that way. And even if you're provoked, try not to get sucked into a confrontation with your difficult colleague: you'll only get worked up even more and probably won't gain anything from it.

- Humour can be a useful tool for deflecting difficult behaviour; but remember, you're not the office clown, so use humour sparingly.

- Some human-resources organisations recommend challenging your colleague about their unreasonable behaviour, but I'm not so sure. If you don't want to get bogged down in constant small rows, or let your colleague know that their bad behaviour bothers you, be careful and pick your battles.

- There is a line between difficult and plain bullying in office life. I'm sure we've all been on the receiving end of behaviour that crosses that line. I remember working in a hotel years ago, and the owner was very difficult—even if I did learn a lot from him. Everyone was afraid of him, and he regularly used to make staff members cry. One Christmas morning when I was on duty, I heard the receptionist crying her eyes out at something he'd said or done. I couldn't believe it—Christmas morning… So I went into his office and said, 'Do you know, one of your staff is crying, and I'm very upset about it.' He didn't say a single word to me; instead, he left the office at 10:15 that morning and he didn't reappear, which was completely out of character, as he was always there. He knew he was in the wrong, even if he didn't want to admit it.

If you think your colleague has crossed a line, it's time to take action. Document any incidents carefully. If necessary, compile a dossier. Keep the focus on the incidents themselves and not on how they made you feel, and approach your boss when you're feeling relatively calm and present your case. If the situation becomes serious, you may well need to seek advice from a trusted colleague, senior member of staff or union representative.

THE FEWER MEETINGS…

'If you had to identify, in one word, the reason why the human race has not achieved, and never will achieve, its full potential, that word would be "meetings".'—Dave Barry

Whether or not you agree with Dave Barry, most of you will have been present at staff meetings of some sort or other during your working lives. In fact, according to *Psychology Today*, many executives will have to spend 40–50 per cent of their time in meetings, which makes me wonder how on earth they get any work done!

We have a management meeting at the Park every Friday at noon, when we look at the past week and what's happened, and look at forecasts for the next ten days and check the rosters, which are done on Tuesday for the following week, to check who needs replacing if they're on holiday—that kind of thing. The meeting takes 35 minutes, 45 tops, and then we get on with our busy days.

The key to efficient meetings is, firstly, to decide if you really, really need one. Don't call one when a quiet word with a few members of the team would have done, or because a meeting has been held every Wednesday morning since 1955. Only call one when it's essential—when you really need people to sit around a table or to contribute by video link. As the renowned economist J. K. Galbraith once said, 'Meetings are indispensable when you don't want to do anything.' So make sure you want to do 'something' at your meeting!

When I read the *Psychology Today* piece I noted what an Ernst and Young executive, Al Pittampalli, had to say about meetings. He describes himself as a 'meeting culture warrior'—brilliant, isn't it? Basically, he tries to change the way people look at, and conduct, meetings, because he thinks we're getting them all wrong. He might well have a point. He thinks they should be used only to uphold a de-

cision that has already been made, or more or less made—
and not actually to make decisions. I think this is excellent
advice. If you gather twelve people around the table to ru-
minate, the chances are that no-one will agree, and you'll
end up with a bit of a mess. Have a clear idea of your deci-
sion and then take views at the meeting to see if any
modifications need to be made.

He also suggested that your meeting should always end
with a plan of action—another way to avoid that 'What is this
all about?' feeling that can accompany a meeting.

If none of the above has put you off, and you decide you
still need a meeting, make sure that you and everyone else
knows what it's about and what it will cover.

- Set an agenda that lays out clearly what the topic of the
  meeting is and the principal points you'll be raising. Keep
  your agenda short and to the point.

- Set a clear time limit and stick to it—don't let meetings
  overrun, because everyone gets exhausted, and nothing
  can be done at all. Make your time limit the minimum
  possible for getting the job done: if you suggest that it will
  be a two-hour meeting, everyone will take two hours! I
  always think that meetings should be no longer than an
  hour. If they drag on they tend to go round in circles. If
  you haven't covered everything, it'll have to wait for the
  next meeting.

- If you'd like people to prepare for the meeting, tell them.
  In fact, people like having a bit of homework to do, because
  it helps them contribute. Send them an e-mail or make a
  phone call to ask them to bring that crucial set of figures
  or that flow chart you'll need to look at.

- Make sure you start the meeting on time, even if not everyone is there. Latecomers can be accommodated, but don't feel you have to give them a summary of what's been happening: it's a waste of valuable time. Just keep going.

- If you're asking someone for their opinion, or to make a presentation, don't allow interruptions and don't interrupt yourself, just listen. When they've finished ask your questions or invite responses.

- There's always someone who dominates meetings, and, without being rude, you want them to pipe down a little! You can just thank them for their contribution and move swiftly on to Mary from accounts. Remember, if it's your meeting, you're in charge. And if you notice people wandering off-message or beginning to get heated about something, move things on. The arguments can be kept for outside the meeting—you have a job to do!

COMMUNICATING IN THE OFFICE

Different workplaces will have different policies about communicating. In a small office or workplace you can simply talk to your colleagues face to face. That's how I try to do things at the Park. I find that problems are resolved much more easily when I get the chance to talk to people. I once had a colleague, though, who insisted on ringing me from his desk ten feet away, which used to drive me crazy, I can tell you.

Of course, I realise that many people work in large offices nowadays, and that group e-mails are a part of working life. I'll be looking at social media in Chapter 9, but, in general, I think you should try to keep the endless e-mails to a minimum—those messages cc'ed to everyone, including the office cat. If you need to send a group e-mail, ask yourself first, 'Do I need to send this?' And only copy in the essential people. Also, try to avoid sending e-mails with jokes in them; many people just don't like them.

While I'm on the subject of communication, I read an interesting article in the business magazine *Forbes* about the problems that can arise in offices between the different generations. One older manager got very upset because her younger colleagues wouldn't answer the phone when she called them: they always texted or e-mailed their replies. Having seen my teenage nieces and nephews in action, I wasn't surprised. They consider it almost bad manners to speak to someone on the phone: it's all texts—'LOL' this and '1daful' that. It's entirely acceptable to them. In fact, calling someone on the phone is considered almost rude! But older people prefer to talk face to face, so try to bear this in mind in your workplace.

Also, try to respect different communication styles: Jenny in goods outwards might feel much more comfortable putting her thoughts on paper than having to phone, so go with it, even if you'd prefer a chat. Similarly, if you feel the impulse to send an e-mail asking for ideas about some new product, why not just go over to your colleague's desk and ask them what they think. Often a conversation will get ideas flowing; sometimes it pays to think outside the box!

TOP OFFICE IRRITANTS

I have to say that researching the many ways in which people get on each other's nerves in offices makes me glad I work in a hotel! Of course, we can also get on each other's nerves, but in different ways. The irritants below might strike a chord with those of you who share those lovely open-plan spaces.

1.

Smelly food. According to a number of surveys, this was the number one irritant. If you're a culprit, think before you buy a burger for lunch.

2.

People complaining about feeling sick. Fed up with that moaner beside you with a headache? Suggest nicely that they take a painkiller or, better still, a little lie-down in the boardroom so you can get on with your work.

3.

People having loud phone conversations that the entire office can hear. They might not be aware that they're being that loud, so maybe mention it when you have a quiet moment.

4.

Hogging the office stapler. I know, it can be irritating when you go to use your stapler or hole punch, only to find that Mary has borrowed it and not given it back. You can certainly label your stapler with your name, but this kind of childish behaviour might not make you terribly popular. Why not put it somewhere Mary will be unlikely to find it? And if you're a Mary: when borrowing something, remember to give it back!

5.

Being late. You know the feeling when you're waiting to get a meeting under way and John rushes in and throws a pile of files on the table. 'Sorry I'm late, the bus took ages,' 'The M50 was a nightmare,' etc. People like John are the bugbear of many an office. Ignore them and get your meeting and your work under way.

6.

Failure to share biscuits. If you get a nice box of chocolates as a thank you, it's a lovely gesture to share them with your colleagues. There's nothing more cheering than a nice bit of chocolate and a cup of tea in the afternoon. I had a colleague who regularly did an ice-cream run for the staff on hot summer days, which cheered everyone up.

7.

Quoting out loud from Facebook and Twitter or sending silly YouTube videos. Quite apart from the fact that doing this will make you look as if you have nothing to do, it's also a pain for people who are trying to concentrate on their work.

On a more positive note, planning small celebrations is a nice gesture in an office. Get someone to make a list of significant dates, such as birthdays, and keep an ear out for occasions like the passing of exams or driving tests, so you can organise tea and cake and a card. Other little ideas are a soup or baking group, where everyone takes a turn bringing in soup or a nice cake for people in the office. Some offices like to have group outings or charity runs to get everyone together in a different context. I have a friend who goes on a golf outing with the office once a year. He doesn't play golf, but everyone dresses up in golf gear and has a bit of fun.

Anything like that really helps to boost office morale. At the Park, we always organise a holiday for the members of staff every year when the hotel is closed.

Most importantly, enjoy yourself. It's not always possible, and many of us have difficult jobs, but we work for a reason—to earn money, certainly, but hopefully also because it's fulfilling and productive. As Henry Ford said, 'There is joy in work. There is no happiness except in the realisation that we have accomplished something.'

The ancient art of grooming:

HOW TO LOOK YOUR BEST
ON EVERY OCCASION

'You can never be overdressed or overeducated.'
—*Oscar Wilde*

I WAS at half-nine Mass in Kenmare the other day, and, apart from the fact that it's a religious occasion, I find it interesting to spot how people look and dress on one of the few truly formal events left. I have a little game where I award bonus points for good appearance. An altar boy who wears the right shoes—he gets two bonus points. And his mother gets more than two bonus points for getting him to wear proper shoes, because they look so much better under the soutane than a great big pair of trainers. I know that God wouldn't mind how people dress, but it's a formal occasion. I also award bonus points for washed hair—can there be anything worse than greasy hair?—and for neat and tidy dress. I can see that the days are past when women and men wore hats to Mass, or wore their Sunday suit, but I don't like baggy jackets, trainers and clothes with creases in them.

Of course, I recognise that times have changed and that many of the rules that governed what I wore growing up don't exist any more, and that's generally fine. But there are a few core rules for dressing that I insist on.

- Absolutely no sleepwear. God invented it for bedtime only, not for doing the shopping in Tesco. A friend of mine saw a young man queueing for coffee recently dressed in a onesie!

- Wear your clothes as they were meant to be worn, unless you work in the fashion business. The fashion for wearing jumpers backwards—I don't really understand that. I saw a woman recently who was wearing her cardigan with the buttons down the back, and I couldn't work out if she was coming or going! When it's a design situation and you're wearing a Chanel jumper, that's fine; but the fact that people are wearing their ordinary clothes back to front, or hanging off them—I have to say that I don't get what it's all about. This may make me sound like a bit of an old fuddy-duddy, but I can't see too many people with their trousers hanging off them getting into medical school. Casual is all well and good, but there's a time and a place for it. My belief is that you should dress appropriately for every occasion. Your clothes should be in good condition, even if they're old—no holes, stains or creases—and you should be clean and tidy, with your hair brushed and your nails, hair and teeth clean.

THE BASICS: HAIR, TEETH AND NAILS

Speaking of hair, teeth and nails, male grooming is no longer a dirty word, and the shelves full of such products prove it. Having said that, I keep things fairly simple. I use soap and water, and maybe the odd touch of a product I get in America called Lubriderm, a moisturiser with a sun protection factor of 15. I don't wear aftershave, because the guests don't like it, and it can transfer to cups and saucers, leaving a nasty aftertaste. I never wear make-up, except when they make me put a bit of powder on my nose when I'm filming, to prevent shine.

The only time I ever had a make-over, if you can call it that, is when I was nabbed by a sales assistant at Bergdorf's in New York, when I was working there. Tom Ford had a new line, and the man was only dying to try it out on me. 'I'll do a great job on you,' he promised me, putting tiny blobs of cream under my eyes. 'You have lovely skin,' he complimented me. 'What do you use?' I was mortified to admit to using only the aforementioned Lubriderm and maybe a bit of Nivea.

I'm happy to get the basics right, even if I've never entirely caught on to the new trends in male grooming. Nonetheless, I came across a nice article on male grooming in the Indian men's magazine *MensXP*, and I think their advice could apply to men the world over. It's been a long time since a slick of Brylcreem did the trick! Their list of no-nos includes 'repulsive feet', hair in the wrong places, too much cologne, not enough hair-washing and not wearing sunscreen. All fairly sensible. I'm not sure I could go the whole hog and have a pedicure, as they recommend, but I agree with them that 'there is no excuse for dirt-filled claws and exceptionally long nails.' The same goes for unwanted hair, gentlemen. There's no need to wax yourselves as smooth as a baby, but trimming nose and ear hair is a must, as is keeping your eyebrows in check. Most barbers will offer a helping hand here, so use the service, particularly when you get to a certain age.

Now, I can't profess to be an expert on women's appearance, but it's true that, as a rule, they take care of themselves a little bit better than we men do. They take more pride in their appearance, I think, and it's perfectly acceptable for them to have regular beauty treatments. I don't think most women would be likely to have the 'dirt-filled claws' mentioned above! Apparently, people find long, elaborately painted nails off-putting in office situations, and I have to agree. At the Park we don't allow bright hair colours, because our clientele is fairly conservative, so it really depends on where you work. If you work in a hair salon I'm sure it's perfectly fine, but make sure it's appropriate for the occasion. I think the general rules should be that less is more, and to keep it simple—no need to slather on the foundation. Keep your nails clean, your hair and teeth brushed, your make-up subtle, and hold off on the fake tan.

And on the subject of teeth, even though people's teeth as a whole have improved a lot because of modern dentistry, and that's brilliant, I think it's gone a bit too far the other way, with people walking around with tombstones in their mouths. They look like the doggy dentures ads on the television!

PERSONAL HYGIENE

The biggest thing you can do for yourself on the personal-grooming front is to wash yourself. It sounds obvious, but you'd be surprised, although things have certainly improved in recent years. It used to be the case that the local young people would come to be interviewed at the Park, and their parents would have them terrified about working here, so they'd come in in a ball of sweat! I used to have to pull members of the staff aside and give them a bottle of deodorant quite regularly. I'd say, 'See that now? You have to use that. No-one will tell you, only Francis Brennan. Your girlfriend won't tell you, your mother and father won't tell you, nobody. I'm the only one who'll tell you that you need to use that.' Years later they come back and say thanks.

Perhaps you might not be a fan of the direct approach when it comes to a colleague with BO, but you might need to steel yourself: we've all worked with someone who doesn't pay close enough attention to their personal hygiene, and it can be a real headache. It really is a difficult subject to broach, as, very often, the person isn't aware of the situation.

However, I wouldn't recommend the route a teacher friend of mine told me about. An exchange teacher came from abroad to the school, which was in inner-city Dublin, and she had an unfortunate personal hygiene problem. The other staff members didn't dare broach it with her and instead just sat at a safe distance in the staff room. The kids didn't hold back, though: when she left, one of them had a T-shirt printed for her with *The bang o' dah'* printed on it! Fortunately, she had no idea what it meant.

If you want to be tactful I like the approach recommended by an article in the *Guardian*. Their expert suggests a 'compliment sandwich', a term I just love. It means taking the problematic co-worker to one side, telling them something great about themselves, then getting to the BO point, before finishing on a positive note. So you could say, 'We just love how you're handling the X account, Mary, but...' Jump right in then, but end by saying, 'Of course, we're very happy with all your hard work...' According to the same expert, women are quicker to take hints, such as a gift of a deodorant, but men need to be told straight out!

If you think you might have a BO problem, and you shower regularly, of course it's upsetting, in which case see your GP. It's possible you might have an underlying medical problem.

LOVELY LOCKS

By this I mean the hair on your head and your facial hair. I've no objection to long hair on a man; it really depends on the quality of the hair. If a man has a good head of thick hair it can look great. It's an individual choice, and not every man has to opt for the short back and sides.

Personally, I like my hair a little bit longer. When I go for a haircut I get it trimmed by a lovely young woman, Trish, in Kenmare. I used to get my hair cut in New York when I was on business. In fact, I had a woman here in the office who used to say, 'Mr Brennan goes to New York to have his hair cut.' But Mr Brennan never, ever went to New York to have his hair cut: he got his hair cut in New York if he happened to be there already! She made it sound as if I hired a private plane in order to get a haircut! But the beauty of a good hairdresser, one that you know, is that they know what you like, and you get the job done just the way you want it.

I also have no objection at all to a beard, if it's kept properly: you don't want to look like Neanderthal Man. I always tell the male staff in the hotel that it's very difficult to start growing a beard in July, during the high season, because you look like the wreck of the *Hesperus* until it grows properly! And the other thing to remember is that you'll have to wear one of those hair nets over it if you work in a kitchen, which isn't a great look, and it creates an instant hygiene problem.

Trim it regularly and keep it neat is my advice. No desert-island beards, please!

BLING: JEWELLERY AND WATCHES

I always remember that, in the late sixties, I bought a chronograph watch in O'Reilly's pawn shop, near Sheriff Street in Dublin. I saved for weeks and weeks and eventually scraped together the 37 shillings I needed. I came home in triumph and showed it off. My father thought I was mad altogether. He'd given me a watch, which he thought was perfectly good, for my Confirmation, and he just couldn't understand why I'd want two watches. I still have it.

Nowadays, there's something of a renaissance in watch-wearing. They fell out of favour when mobile phones came in, but now they're seen as fashion items, rather than as time-keepers, and the mid-range models are growing in popularity, that is, watches that cost between €300 and €500. Many men's designers now produce ranges, in much the same way that women's designers produce handbags. It's a little bit of haute couture for a fraction of the price of an outfit.

This may seem obvious to my generation, but, for those who aren't used to wearing a watch, if you're right-handed it's normal to wear the watch on your left hand, and vice versa. And I know the style now is to turn everything on its head, but if you have a sports watch—one of those diver's watches that allows you to go 300 metres under water, in case you ever need to—it looks better with casual wear, whereas a dressier watch, or even an antique one, looks far better with a suit.

CLOTHING ESSENTIALS

I can't honestly profess to be any kind of an expert on what works for women. To me, the right outfit means basically a suit and tie. Our guests and any wedding couple coming to the Park don't want to be met by either John or myself in a jumper. John meets guests at Dromquinna Manor in a jumper and open-necked shirt, because it's a more relaxed place. This doesn't mean sloppy, just more casual.

Now, I know that not everyone will want or even need to wear a suit and tie. It depends on the occasion. Some people don't need to dress formally in the workplace, but there are certain basics: no shorts or flip-flops, no cut-off jeans, no revealing clothes—and this is so no matter where you work.

For women, I think skirt length can be a big issue. If you work in a solicitor's firm or a bank you're going to need knee-length or below—and if you're of a certain age, ladies, no minis, please! There's an age for wearing them, and it's not forty-five!

Necklines can be another issue for women in the workplace. Clearly, it's not okay to reveal too much, which reminds me of a joke I heard once. A young woman was going to Mass, and she put on a top she'd wondered about for a bit—was it a touch too revealing? She decided it wasn't, and off she went. She was marching up the aisle to her seat, when the usher stopped her.

'Excuse me, madam, where are you going?'

Taken aback, she said, 'I'm going to Mass.'

'Not like that you're not,' he replied. 'Your blouse is a bit see-through.'

The woman was outraged. 'Excuse me, I have a divine right...' she sputtered.

To which he replied, 'Indeed. You have a divine right, and a divine left as well.'

The moral of the story is to be discreet, I think! Revealing clothing is not for the office.

Joking aside, I think women have a little bit more leeway than men when it comes to clothing, both in casual and in formal wear, and I think they can have a little bit more fun with it and bend the rules a bit. Of course, in the office, gaudy patterns and odd fabrics won't work, but women can use colour more than men, I think. They can accent a sober suit with a bright-pink shirt, or a navy-and-white stripe. They can get away with wearing dark-coloured jeans in any number of styles, paired with a pretty blouse, and it looks so much more respectable than the male equivalent of baggy jeans and a T-shirt. Women can wear any kind of dress, whether it's a shirt dress or a wrap or a tea dress, and it doesn't have to cost them a fortune. And the range of shoe styles that women can wear with, say, office wear, is so much broader; although I would caution against a very high heel, unless at a nightclub. If you avoid loud prints, which can look cheap, you can actually put together an outfit at a fraction of the cost of a man's. Lucky women!

When it comes to clothing basics, just as with hair and nails, clothes should be clean and stain-free, and if they crease easily, iron them. You'd be amazed what a difference it makes. T-shirts should be clean. Where you choose to buy them will depend on your budget. I work at one New York department store sometimes, promoting Irish tourism, and every T-shirt there is $229 plus tax. I suppose it's a question of quality—they're double stitched, and the arms don't barrel out, and I'm sure they don't go baggy, as those from some clothes chains would—but there can't be too many of us with that amount of cash to spend on a T-shirt.

TIES

I'm a tie collector, and I freely admit to having far too many of them. Once, I had about forty ties I didn't want, and I gave them to the local charity shop. (There were some very nice ones in the bunch, I have to say!) One day I was driving from Kenmare to Kilgarvan, and didn't I see one of my ties holding shut a farmer's gate! I thought it was very clever: the tie wouldn't break, and he'd probably got it for a euro—and I was tickled pink at the idea of a Givenchy tie holding a gate closed.

Tie styles, like those for suits and shirts, vary; but as I discovered when I was researching this book, ties have a long history. Apparently they've been worn for thousands of years in one form or another, but they really took off when Louis XIII saw the Croatian mercenaries he'd hired wearing something he'd come to call a 'cravat', during the Thirty Years' War. Louis took a shine to the little scarves and made them mandatory at court—and the tie was born. However, like many of the traditions we now see as normal, the tie itself dates from Victorian times. According to the website www.bows-n-ties.com, 'It is said that this modern necktie knot was invented by British horsemen who used this knot to tie a scarf around their neck while holding the reins of four horses in the other.'

The fashion is now for narrow ties, which I don't much like. When you're that bit older and have a bit of a tummy it doesn't look right. You look like a cowboy! The opposite extreme is the big, wide 'kipper' tie, which can make you look like a footballer. The key, I think, is to match your tie size and the knot you use to the shirt collar you've chosen (see below, p. 168).

I have an app on my phone on tie knots, in order to show the staff at the hotel, and I find it very handy. Personally, I use a Windsor knot, with the tie down and the button open: it's a no-no. The Windsor knot—called after King Edward VIII—stays put all day.

According to Thomas Fink and Yong Mao, two Cambridge researchers, there are no fewer than eighty-five ways to tie a tie, which they revealed in their book of the same name in 1999. I think there are really just three you need to know:

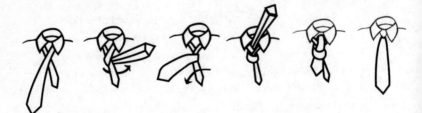

The *four-in-hand* is the classic knot you'd have learned to tie in school, if you had a school tie. You drape the tie around your neck, with the narrow end coming halfway down the length of the wide end, then you flip the wide end over the narrow one once, twice, then up through the loop you've created, and hey presto!

The **half-Windsor** is a bit more complicated. You have to wrap the wide end around the narrow end, then down through the loop created, so that it's a nice triangle. Once you have that done you'll do it again and then you'll have a nice knot to adjust. This classic tie style is great for any kind of shirt collar.

The **Windsor** is a step up from this. You loop the wide end around the narrow end a number of times to get a nice fat knot. You'll often see this tie on formal shirts in morning suits, where the collar is quite wide, or 'spread'. There are any number of videos online that can show you how to tie your tie, if you need a little extra help. One site I like is www.life-hacker.com, and it includes instructions on how to tie a bow tie, if you're feeling particularly brave.

When it comes to the tie pattern, I think you can afford to play around a little, as it's the one embellishment we men really have; but I'm not a fan at all of novelty ties. I wouldn't dream of wearing one with leprechauns or that kind of thing on it. Classic is best, I think. Clip-on ties are an absolute no-no, unless you want to look like you're making your First Holy Communion!

As to length, according to the men's style bible, the magazine *GQ*, your tie should drop to the level of your belt—no shorter and no longer. Which is all well and good, but if you're a taller man, or if, as the *Wall Street Journal* puts it, you have a 'bigger belly', you'll need a longer tie. The *WSJ* also advises men to wear a shorter tie with the skinnier suits that are fashionable at the moment, and also to bear in mind the kind of knot you'll be using. If, like me, you use a Windsor knot, this uses more fabric, so if you don't want your tie resting on your tummy you might want a longer one. As with everything, try your tie on before you buy it, to see how it looks.

Monday in Gieves and Hawkes

To some, a cummerbund might seem like an old-fashioned touch, but I think they help to finish a certain type of evening outfit. Nowadays, of course, they all have elasticated backs and are simple to put on. Never one to take the easy way out, I have a proper long one that I wrap around myself a number of times. Naturally, it comes with a nice story.

I bought a suit in Louis Féraud a good many years ago. It was a lovely burgundy and gold, with a short waiter's jacket, and I wanted a cummerbund to go with it. I happened to be in London, so one rainy Monday morning I ran up Savile Row and into Gieves and Hawkes, the gentlemen's outfitters, because I was sure they'd have one. The minute I stepped across the threshold I thought, I shouldn't be here. It was the kind of men's shop where everything was in a glass case.

I was about to make a hasty exit when a salesman stepped out. 'Good morning. Can I help you?'

I took a deep breath, feeling completely out of my depth. 'I'm looking for a cummerbund, but a proper one,' I said.

He looked thoughtful. 'Hmm... a cummerbund. It's a long, long time since I saw a proper cummerbund. I'll check with Roger.'

It was getting worse. I managed a 'Thanks,' mortified and only dying to run out of the shop as the assistant called out, 'Roger, would we have a cummerbund in stock?'

Roger appeared and said, 'Try Milisha upstairs. Come up and I'll show you a shortcut.'

I was delighted with myself: I was to meet Milisha upstairs and talk about cummerbunds! I followed Roger to the back of the shop and up a set of stairs to the next floor. When I arrived the only two customers were an American man and his wife; they were with the salesman, who had a big ledger open in front of him. They were clearly discussing an entire outfit, but the relaying of information amused me. The Gieves and Hawkes man would ask, 'Double cuffs?' and the woman would ask her husband, 'Double cuffs?' He'd reply, 'Yes, double cuffs,' and she'd say, 'Double cuffs,' to the assistant, and he'd write it in the ledger.

This went on for the next twenty minutes. The two men couldn't talk to each other: it had to go through the wife, and the process took an age. While I was standing around, I noticed that everything in the department was beefeater jackets or army coats with lapels and badges. Suddenly, the penny dropped: 'militia', not 'Milisha'. It was the uniform department. Thank God I hadn't opened my mouth, I thought, and asked to speak to Milisha!

Eventually, the salesman closed the ledger and said goodbye to the two Americans. 'I'm sorry about the delay,' he said.

'Oh, that's fine. I'm looking for a cummerbund,' I explained. 'You know, like Fred Astaire wore in *Singin' in the Rain*. (In fact, he didn't: it was Gene Kelly. I misremembered, clearly aiming for Astaire's beautiful presentation.)

'Oh, I'm not sure,' the salesman said, opening drawers, out of which he took ancient plastic bags. Then he said, 'Hold on a minute. I think you're in luck.' And he pulled a long length of fabric out and began unrolling it, walking up the shop floor until he was ten yards away!

I suddenly wondered if I had to buy it by the yard—'I'll have a yard of cummerbund, please'—and I have to say, I felt like a complete eejit. First 'Milisha' and now this! It would probably cost about £600.

Finally, I managed 'It's just what I want… but is it very pricey?'

'Oh, I don't know,' he said, 'I'll just check,' and he put on his glasses and peered at the little tag attached to it. 'Oh, it's in old money. I'll have to work it out for you.' He went to the cash desk and tapped the amount into a calculator, before announcing, 'It's 2 pounds 7 shillings. You're very lucky: this was priced in about 1935.'

I couldn't believe my luck—maybe it had been worth the embarrassment after all. 'I'll take it, so. Thank you very much.'

I still have my cummerbund, but it's not easy to put on. I have to wrap it around me once, then lean against the wall and wrap it around another ten times or so, until it's finally done. I think the elasticated ones are probably a bit easier after all.

A SUIT IS A MAN'S BEST FRIEND

There's something about me and farmers. I wear lots of suits, and I don't wear them out too quickly, so every so often I look through them and give some to my mother, who passes them on to a farmer in Co. Sligo. I'll bet there's a Louis Féraud suit going up and down ploughing a field there this morning!

I don't have them made to measure, although I know many men who swear by this in order to get the very best fit. It's a good option but an expensive one. I buy them off the peg, because I buy them all over the world and can choose from a good selection. I know the cut immediately, because I'm used to looking for it. I look for a Van Gils or a Burberry—all nice suits made of good quality fabric.

With suits, styles vary and fashions come and go. For example, the double-breasted suit is considered a bit of an 1980s relic at the moment, but it'll probably come back into fashion. And leg lengths vary: at the moment, the shorter look is fashionable, with the leg stopping just above the shoe. I prefer mine a bit longer. Suit fashions tend to go in cycles: I have suits that I would wear tomorrow that I bought in F. X. Kelly twenty-five years ago.

I always look for a *continental suit*—one with no 'vent' (small flap) in the back—because the line is nice and structured, and also it doesn't crease as easily.

Vents were invented, if you'll excuse the pun, at a time when men rode on horseback, as it gave them more freedom of movement. It's true that you can't move about in a continental suit quite as much, but with a single, **centre vent**, if you're wearing the jacket when you sit down it creases unless you pull it down under your rear end. The other thing about a centre vent is that it can look unflattering: if the vent is flapping open, the suit's too small for you. I have one or two suits with centre vents but only because I particularly like the fabric.

Occasionally I'll wear a suit with **two vents**. If you don't have one, it has a vent on each side of the back of the jacket, just above your hips, creating a kind of flap. I'm wearing one as I write, because, again, I like the material. The two-vent suit is better suited to the larger man, as the two vents can give a slimming look, but be careful if you're blessed with a large posterior: the double vent can flap up and draw attention to it.

I've only one **double-breasted suit**, because it's in a nice material, and when I'm looking for something a little bit different I try to play around with the collar style. I was at a dinner the other night and I wore a suit with a mandarin collar on it. It cost me a fortune when I bought it twenty-five years ago—I'd say the equivalent of about €900 today—but I still wear it, and it's still admired. At least four people came up to me and said, 'I love your jacket.' I really think you can't beat quality.

The best colour to buy is probably dark grey, particularly if you're not a regular suit-wearer or are on a tight budget: this colour will be presentable just about anywhere. A pin stripe is for City financiers or Tory politicians, and it can make you look unnaturally tall and thin if you're in any way tall and thin to begin with!

Also, if you're a slender man, buy a suit in a heavier fabric. If you're bigger, go lighter. And while three-button suits have their moments, particularly if you're a taller man and the top button doesn't stop at your neck, the classic look is for two buttons, as it's easier to wear.

When you're buttoning up your jacket, don't button up all the buttons, because you'll look as if you're squeezed into the suit. Neither should you leave your jacket flapping in the wind. Button the top button only.

When it comes to sizing, as a general rule I always buy a suit a size too big, because it makes me looks smaller, although I freely admit that this might not work with the new slimmer-cut styles of suit. Measure your chest width and arm length using a tape measure and then experiment by trying on a number of suit jackets to see what works. I feel that you shouldn't want to buy it at your exact size or a size too small, because you'll look squeezed into it. Also, you'll have a phone and pen, which will add inches to the 'circle', that is, your shape in the suit. I have to add that many of us men just hate asking for help in shops: we want to get in and out as quickly as possible. But if you don't want to end up with an ill-fitting, expensive mistake, ask the assistant for advice.

I don't open the pockets of any of my suits, because if I do I'm tempted to put all kinds of stuff into them. As a rule, you should carry only a pen, some business cards——there's a pocket for these in the bottom left-hand of your suit——and your mobile phone. Thankfully, many of the mobiles nowadays are not of the brick variety and so shouldn't make your suit baggy. And you can always use your man bag (see below, p. 172).

SUIT CARE

This is how I take care of my suits: when I come home from work I put the trousers in the trouser press, and I hang the jacket in the bathroom to breathe. When I shower in the morning the steam takes off the creases. That evening I put the suit back in the wardrobe. I find that this really works for me, and many of my suits have lasted me years.

A CRISP WHITE SHIRT

I must have about fifteen unopened shirts as well as about forty on the go. If my dad were around now he'd ask me why I need more than fifty shirts! I'm a bit of a shirt collector, and I have all kinds of styles, but I like cotton, for the quality and freshness, though I understand that they need careful ironing. Cotton is also more breathable, so you might take this into account if you're working in a stuffy office. If you're all for ease of care, buy a cotton mix shirt, which is easier to iron.

If you're new to the world of formal shirts, before you go anywhere measure yourself for your shirt size. Shirts are measured according to your neck size—15 inch, 16½ inch etc.—and your arm length, so get your tape measure out. Once you've measured yourself (the measure goes around your neck, and from your shoulder to your wrist bone) and worked out your size, all you need to do is to think about which of the many collar and shirt styles you'd like to wear.

To start with the *collar*, there are a number of styles: point, spread, button-down, cutaway—the list is seemingly endless, which prompted the *Wall Street Journal* to ask,

'What's happened to men's collars? There are now not just spread collars but medium spreads and extreme spreads, and not just button-down collars but abbreviated button-down collars and short, rounded button-down collars.' It can get confusing! The reason for all these changes, according to the *WSJ*, is that collar styles that were out of fashion have now been reintroduced. One such is the detachable collar, which might be familiar to you from Hollywood films of the 1930s. Also, the 'slimming down of the male silhouette' means that smaller collars work better.

Personally, I always wear a 'point' collar: just straight down—a classic style that men have worn since the turn of the century, because it works so well with a tie. Some of the newer styles are meant to be worn without ties, or, in the case of the 'cutaway', with a tie with a huge knot—our footballers again!

A 'spread' collar is one with rounded ends and a wider space between the points of the collar, in order to accommodate a larger tie. It's now very popular with businessmen and the like, and the rounded ends are flattering.

An 'abbreviated spread' collar is a short collar with a wide gap between the ends; it's popular with the newer slim-fit suits and skinny ties.

As to the *style* of your shirt, you can now pick from a whole range of styles in order to flatter your body type. Thomas Pink has just introduced the 'athletic fit' to cater for a man with wide shoulders and a narrow waist. Would that we could all be so lucky! I like classic styles myself, but try not to buy baggy shirts, even if you have a bit of a tummy, because the bagginess will only exaggerate it. Instead, try to find a shirt that fits you comfortably but doesn't billow like a sail. Most of the slim-fit styles you see nowadays will work, but make sure you try on lots of them, as they won't all be the same. Super slim-fits are for skinny hipsters.

When it comes to *tie-wearing* I'm a traditionalist myself. For example, I never wear a tie on a button-down shirt, because the shirts are casual. The Americans were the first to start wearing button-down shirts, and they were produced in a lot of colours, unlike the sober white business shirt. But then someone produced a white button-down shirt and, before you knew it, people started wearing ties with them. I'm not a fan. For a start, you can't squeeze a tie into a button-down collar, at least not without missing the bus while you fiddle with your buttons, which you've had to open. And then you have to face the spectacle of a lumpy collar where the tie won't quite fit. Having said that, I believe that many designers now produce button-down shirts that will take a tie, and I saw a picture of Warren Buffett wearing one recently— what's the world coming to!

I like a button-down collar for casual wear, because the collar sits perfectly under a suit jacket if I'm not wearing a tie. Otherwise the collar is up high and sticking out, and I have to keep pulling it down under my jacket.

I always wear white dress shirts at the hotel, because I think they look just right; but when I'm going away on a long trip I'll throw in two blue shirts, because they'll work for me as either casual or formal shirts, in case there's no laundry in the hotel. Otherwise I wear only white shirts. I don't like wearing colours as I don't think it looks professional.

When it comes to *cuffs*, make sure your cuff is resting on your wrist bone: any shorter and you'll need a longer sleeve; any longer and the shirt's too big for you. I like French cuffs, the kind you fold back and hold with cuff links. They present properly and look better. I like wearing cuff links, because they really accent style. I like personalising mine with my initials. You can also get them made out of old Irish coins or with the logo of the golf club on them. There are all kinds of ways to wear them, and they make great presents. However, I'm not a fan of tie embellishments, such as pins, because I think they make you look like a poker player!

BEST FOOT FORWARD

We've already looked at clothing appropriate for the occasion, but what about the feet? I know that some of the younger lads will have a go at wearing trainers with a suit, but I'm not of that ilk. I can see that Converse could add a certain something to an old man's suit—if you're a hipster—but, personally, I think there's nothing like a polished set of brogues to set off that suit. The shoes should be classic, with no shiny materials, no suede, no pointy toes and no block heels. I know that some men wear loafers with a suit, but it makes me shudder, to be honest.

And the colour rules? Well, you wouldn't wear matching brown shoes with a brown suit, unless you want to look like you've stepped out of the 1970s; but you could wear a different shade of brown—maybe a tan colour or oxblood. With a brown suit, I'd say black brogues would be a no-no. With a black suit, black is your only man, unless you're hoping to make some kind of a fashion statement, and the same goes for dark-grey suits: a black brogue is definitely best. Only break the fashion rules if you know what you're doing!

THE MAN BAG

According to the *Telegraph*, a survey reported that more than half of men carry a 'man bag', and the style of this varies. There's the practical rucksack you see everywhere nowadays, which I don't particularly like, unless you're a student, although a suede or leather version can look smart as well as practical. There's the briefcase, which, thankfully, isn't the snap-closed model we used to use; it can be in nice, soft leather, as can the leather satchel, which is both attractive and practical, having plenty of room for tablet computers and newspapers. Then, heaven help us, there's the 'man clutch', which speaks for itself and can serve no useful purpose, as it seems to be barely larger than an envelope, as well as looking just plain silly with a suit. Last but not least there is the plastic bag, which can surely be no man's friend.

If you're looking for a bag that is both smart and practical I think it has to be one of soft leather, in a neutral colour that will work with more or less anything you wear. It also has to be big enough to fit the kind of things men carry around with them—glasses, pens, tablet computers, mobile phones, newspapers, headphones—but not too big, because you'll be tempted to fill it with all kinds of stuff, and you'll look as if you're off to the gym.

So there you have it—my sartorial advice. I think the main things to remember about clothes are that you should enjoy wearing them, have a little bit of fun with them and try to look as presentable as you can. My job in the hotel means that I've been able to indulge my love of a good suit and a freshly ironed white shirt. It doesn't have to be expensive or designer, just nicely put together, comfortable and with a little bit of thought behind it.

Eating out

'There is no sincerer love than the love of food.'
—*George Bernard Shaw*

NOT SO LONG ago, dining out was a big deal. It involved either lunch in a country hotel or, for the lucky few, one of the classic restaurants of the time, such as Jammet's in Nassau Street in Dublin——a proper French restaurant that served classic cuisine like steak tartare and coquilles St-Jacques, and whose waiters were trained for three years before being let loose on the customers. According to the food critic Tom Doorley, one classic Jammet's recipe began: 'Take one raw boar's head. Remove the ears to cook separately...'

Most Irish people couldn't afford Jammet's and rarely, if ever, ate out. Nowadays, eating out is part of normal life, and with the arrival of the mid-range restaurant it's afford-able to many. It's also a great deal more casual than it used to be. However, it's not fast food, and certain standards need to be observed in order to make eating out more pleasant, but also to respect the waiting staff and the restaurant. But eating out is also supposed to be about en-joyment——about sharing food and time with friends and family, so relax and have fun!

Soup, glorious soup

If you're at all nervous about eating out it might help you to know that one of my most embarrassing faux pas involves food. I was in Vienna at a Skål conference (Skål is the federa-tion of hotel and tourism professionals), and we were staying at the lovely Hotel Bristol after a ten-day tour of Austria. We had just returned from a night at the opera when my friend Brian invited me to lunch the following day with a member of the Viennese aristocracy. I wasn't sure, because I didn't know this lady, but Brian prevailed and, the next day, off we headed into the snowy Austrian countryside.

Now, I have to mention here that on our tour of the country we'd eaten the same dish every single night, without exception: a stew of boiled meat and dumplings, called *knödel*. It's their national dish, and they're very proud of it. But nine days in a row... I thought I was losing my mind.

We arrived at this woman's beautiful home, with electric gates and an imposing driveway, a little way outside Vienna, and when we drove up in our minibus the lady of the house was standing on the front steps in her fur coat to welcome us. Before we sat down to lunch she insisted on showing us her stables and her collection of fine horses and carriages. It turned out that she competed in coach-and-four competitions, the same kind of event Prince Philip used to do. Needless to say, I was completely overawed.

After our visit to the stables we were ushered into the dining room, a beautiful room with lovely furniture and crystal chandeliers. The waiting staff were dressed in black and white. We had an aperitif and then went to the table, as lunch was to be served. I remembered my manners and seated the hostess before going to sit down myself. As I pushed her chair in, the kitchen door opened, and I saw a big tureen being carried in, with dumplings in it, bouncing up and down. Good Lord, more boiled stew and dumplings, I thought. I just couldn't take another meal of boiled stew and dumplings...

I went back around to my seat, but I got a fit of the giggles, managing to hold them in only with great difficulty. And then the waitress, in her wisdom, decided to serve me first, approaching me with the tureen and saying, '*Zuppe*.' At this, I lost my composure completely and started to laugh hysterically, and I couldn't catch my breath. I had to get out of the room, so I fell into the kitchen, through the swing doors, my face bright red and in total convulsions. The chef thought I was having a heart attack and promptly rang for the doctor.

Thankfully, the lady of the house came in and tried to explain to him. 'It's okay, it's only the stew.'

Even though I was flying high on the wings of hysteria I was completely mortified at my display of bad manners. I've never eaten stew and dumplings since…

GROUND RULES

So, you've been invited out for a meal at a nice restaurant and you're greatly looking forward to it. Before we get started, consider a couple of things, namely mobile phones and smoking. I have to say, in the last twelve years we've had only four problems with people using mobiles in the dining room at the Park, so I think people are generally more sensible than you'd think. However, there are a couple of things to bear in mind: mobile phones are not guns in the saloon, and they don't need to be slung onto the table, to be stared at for the rest of the night. I always have a rule when I go out to restaurants that we put away the mobile phones, because I don't want to sit at a table with people playing with them—it'll drive me mad. I don't know how people's heads don't burst! I switch my phone off so that I can fully enjoy my meal and the company. If you're in a restaurant and you absolutely have to take a call, excuse yourself from the table. Say, 'One moment and I'll be back.' It's different if you're in a busy café: there's no problem in taking a call. It's common sense, really.

And as to smoking, the era of indoor smoking has of course passed, but I think it's a bit of a nuisance when people constantly get up from the table to go outside to smoke. You lose the thread of the conversation. It's rude, quite frankly. There's really no nice way of saying it—your best friend won't tell you, but I'll tell you! If you have to go, go just once—no cigarette after every course. Remember, it was considered very bad manners a while ago to smoke between courses in restaurants, so use the same logic when it comes to going outside.

Once the ground rules have been established, you're all set.

A NOTE ON SITTINGS

During the Celtic Tiger era, 'sittings' at restaurants were all the rage, such was the demand for us to go out and spend all our money. And while the practice of 'table-turning' is still common, it really rankles with restaurant-goers. According to a survey in the *Guardian*, it was their biggest complaint. Some diners feel that if they're spending a lot of money in a restaurant, they don't want to suffer being booted out the door at 9 p.m., having come in at only 7:30 p.m. Others consider it part of the territory, particularly at popular restaurants.

The same goes for making reservations. It has become the practice in some restaurants not to accept bookings, which some people don't like. But according to the Restaurants Association of Ireland, people often make reservations and then don't turn up, leaving the restaurant with empty tables, particularly at Christmastime. If you make a reservation but find you can't go, please do consider the restaurant and ring them to cancel it. This applies particularly if you're in a large group, as the restaurant may very well have taken on extra staff to cater for you.

ARRIVING AT THE RESTAURANT

So, your friend has made a reservation for you, or you have, so now you might want to look up the restaurant's website to see what kind of food they offer. If you're lucky enough to be going to a to-die-for, Michelin-starred restaurant you'll probably already have looked at the site so you could salivate over the menu! Most restaurants have a set menu of two or three courses at a fixed price, or *prix fixe*, to use the lingo. Alternatively, you can order à la carte ('from the menu'), choosing what you like. This is generally more expensive.

As to dress codes, most restaurants no longer have a strict code, and you can generally wear whatever makes you feel comfortable. Sometimes it's nice, though, to dress up a little for the occasion, and if you'll be dining at, say, a golf club or a yacht club, check the dress code first. Many clubs insist on a jacket and tie.

When you arrive at the restaurant you'll greet the front-of-house host or hostess, and, if you haven't mentioned it, you'll be asked if you have a reservation, before being shown to your table. I'm always amused at the Park when the waiter says, 'Follow me,' to the guests and they scatter like ducks in a field! They're all over the place. Take it from me: the waiter knows the quickest way to your table, so follow him.

AT THE TABLE

It's very important to treat your waiter with respect: never treat them as someone lesser than yourself. A lot of us were waiters in university—big guys like Donald Trump were probably waiters at one stage! But it's not just that: treating people equally is a core belief for me. And it makes practical sense too. If you're nice to your waiter they will make a special effort to look after you and your fellow guests, and they probably won't go the extra mile if you're rude or unpleasant. Not only that, but you'll look unkind in front of your friends.

Once you've arrived at your table, try not to take ten minutes to sit down, with lengthy discussions: 'You sit here, and I'll sit here.' Just pull out a chair and sit down. When the waiter comes and gives you the menu, say thank you. When browsing the menu try not to spend twenty minutes chatting and then, when the waiter comes to take your order, say, 'Oh, we haven't decided.' It's all about timing if you're a waiter. If the menu is huge I always say quietly, 'Please give us ten minutes.' Also, if the restaurant is child-friendly, something should quickly be put in front of any children in your party.

But don't be afraid to ask, if this isn't the case: hungry children are stressful for you and your fellow diners. Buttered bread will be just the ticket.

DON'T PANIC: YOUR GUIDE TO TABLE SETTINGS

If you're eating in a 'proper' restaurant the array of cutlery, glasses and napkins can be bewildering. Try not to panic—think of all the lovely things you're about to eat! The rule of thumb when it comes to cutlery is to work from the outside in, with cutlery for first courses being on the outside, progressing inwards to the main course on either side of the plate. So:

- On the outside the hors d'oeuvre fork, for your starter, will be on the far left.

- On the far right you'll see a fish knife and, to the left of that, your soup spoon, if there will be a soup course.

- Next in we have, on the left, the main course fork and, on the right, the main course knife—we call them 'joint' knives and forks in the business.

- Above the plate we have a dessert fork and spoon. If there will be any other courses—sorbet or cheese, say—the cutlery will be placed in the order of service, that is, the order in which you'll be eating. Just remember the magic words 'outside in' and you'll be just grand.

- Napkins, in a restaurant, are always folded on a 'cover plate', and when you sit down the waiter may put the napkin on your lap and whip the plate away. You just keep your napkin on your lap—there's no need to tie it around your neck, unless, of course, you're at a lobster restaurant, where you'll generally be provided with a 'bib' for the job. The 'cover plate', or 'charger plate', as they call it in the United States, also marks the space where the main course plate will be placed.

- Wine glasses are to the right of the table setting: a glass each for white wine and for red, and a tumbler for water. The red wine glass is the largest, as red wine has to breathe. If the guest won't be drinking, the waiter will remove the glass so that they don't accidentally serve wine to the guest later. Now you're ready to order!

ORDERING

When it comes to ordering it's useful to know what the waiter is thinking. When they take the order in a certain way they do so to identify person 1, 2, 3, etc. and what they have ordered, so that when the food comes they know where they're going with it. So when they start taking the order try not to jump in: let the waiter do the sequential ordering, and hand back the menu.

If you run out of water during the meal, don't wave a serviette or click your fingers. Catch a waiter's eye and say, 'Excuse me.' Michael Winner used to wave a serviette, Lord have mercy on him, but he only got away with it because he was Michael Winner! The same goes if you want water or bread: catch the waiter's eye, wait for them to come over, and then ask quietly if you can have some water or bread. When it comes to water, you're quite entitled to ask for tap water, rather than the expensive stuff in a bottle. Just say, 'Tap water, please.'

A MENU PRIMER

Of course, restaurant menus aren't written only in French any more, but there are a number of terms on modern menus that might puzzle you. Here is a handy primer.

When it comes to aperitifs (drinks served before the meal), *Kir* is white wine and cassis; *Kir royale* is champagne and cassis. Both make lovely aperitifs, as does a *Mimosa*, which is champagne and orange juice.

Of course, the more adventurous might well opt for a cocktail, such as a *Martini* or a *Bellini*—a mixture of prosecco or champagne and peach juice.

Amuse-bouche literally means 'mouth-amuser' and is a little mouthful that's often served before a meal. You'll often see this on tasting menus.

Bruschetta, an Italian dish, is now fairly widely interpreted, but in the original form it's slices of toasted white bread, such as ciabatta, on which is served a mixture of chopped fresh tomato, red onion and herbs.

Carpaccio is very thin slices of raw meat or fish—tuna or beef are popular—generally served with a sauce.

Ceviche is raw fish cured in citrus, generally lime.

Confit means meat that has been cooked in its own fat. Confit duck is a common term on menus these days.

Crostini are little slices of toasted white bread with a variety of toppings, and they're lovely as canapés for a drinks party.

A **fricassee** is a light 'stew' of meat or vegetables, finely chopped and added to a stock or wine mixture—great if you have leftover turkey at Christmastime.

Jus is not gravy but actually the meat's own juices served with it, but not thickened. A **reduction**, on the other hand, is generally red wine added to a pan with, say, shallots and cooked until it reduces to a thick sauce, with butter added at the end.

Osso buco is veal shank cooked very slowly, so that the marrow melts.

Steak cooking is a bit of a minefield, and indeed most restaurant complaints involve the incorrect cooking of steak. If you want it **blue** it just means searing the outside of the meat for ten seconds and then serving—for the adventurous! **Rare** means that the centre of the steak should be nice and red and still cool. **Medium rare** is when the steak is cooked for three minutes on each side and is still red, but just in the centre. **Medium** means that it's pink in the centre, and **well done** is brown all the way through.

DESSERT

I love the quotation 'Life is short. Eat dessert first.' It's my favourite part of the meal! Terms you might have come across are **semifreddo, parfait, pavé, baklava** and **panna cotta**.

Semifreddo means 'half cold' in Italian and is a cross between a mousse and an ice cream, made with cream, and not with eggs and milk, as in ice cream. Yum! It's very handy if you want to make it at home, because you don't have to use an ice-cream maker.

A **parfait** is really the French version of this, using a sugar syrup heated to a high temperature.

The magazine *Taste* refers to a **pavé** as a 'rectangular-shaped, frosted and layered sponge cake dessert filled with sweet ingredients such as buttercream and coated with a frosting.' A pavé can also be savoury, as it really refers to the shape of the dish: it means 'cobblestone' in French!

Panna cotta is an Italian favourite, a mixture of cream, milk and sugar 'cooked' with a vanilla pod, to which gelatin is added to make a mixture between a jelly and a mousse.

A **baklava** is one of those delicious Middle Eastern pastries made of layers of filo-like pastry, usually filled with honey and nuts.

WINE

When you've ordered your food you'll then need to consult the wine list to find a nice bottle or glass to go with it. Nowadays, people know a lot more about wine than they used to. The regular columns in the Sunday papers and helpful tips in supermarkets and off-licences mean that we are all wine experts these days. That's brilliant if you're eating out, because it gives you more confidence about ordering. Also, a lot of restaurants have tidied up their wine lists and offer just six reds and six whites. That's very acceptable for a local place and makes it easier for the customer to select a wine they like. If the owner has taken the time to research their list, they don't need to be too fussy about having a large quantity of stock. Maybe you'd prefer a Merlot to a Cabernet Sauvignon, but the owner will generally select wines for the general public, as they know that many people are looking for a wine in the €30–40 region. We won't go into mark-ups in this book, as that's another day's work!

At the Park we have more than four hundred wines on our list, but we'd be one of the few remaining places in the country to do so. We have the list split up into regions, so if you like Sancerre you go to that section and pick from a selection and so on. This is all well and good if you know what you're about as a wine lover, and the wine waiter will always advise you. However, if you're just a general wine lover, be guided by price. If you're not that into wine, you don't need to spend €100, as most wines are of reasonable quality these days.

When it comes to the top end of wine buying, I'd buy wine at auctions—the Metropole Hotel in Cork has closed, but they had some lovely wines in their cellar, some of which we bought for the Park. Also, we have one or two wine merchants who guide us. For example, if I'm buying Château Pétrus at €400–500 a bottle, I'm not going to want to buy a case of it: I wouldn't sell more than a bottle or two a year. A good wine merchant will say, 'I've got a case. Would you like four bottles?' Château Pétrus is an *occasion* bottle of wine! Also, from a business point of view, I can't afford to have €300,000 worth of wine in the cellar.

TIPS FOR ORDERING WINE

- If you're ordering wine with your meal, don't be afraid to tell the wine waiter, 'I've a budget of €50 for wine. What do you have that's special in that price range?'

- Ask the waiter what wine would go well with your chosen meal. 'I'm having steak. Can you recommend a wine to go with it?' Or 'This New Zealand Sémillon, would it be nice with my monkfish?' It's all about having confidence, and that means having the confidence to ask when you *don't* know or aren't familiar with what's on offer. You're the customer and spending your hard-earned cash in their restaurant, so don't be afraid to ask.

- Remember, if you're with a group of people try to select a wine that most people will like—no massive, robust red for Granny, who'd just like a sip of Chardonnay!

- If you can't pronounce the name of the wine, don't worry. You don't have to have a degree in Spanish or French to order it. Simply point to it on the list and allow the waiter to take the lead—they'll be used to it and will be happy to step in. You can just point and say, 'This one, please,' and the waiter will say, 'The Saint-Émilion—very nice,' or words to that effect!

- When the wine arrives at your table, check the label to make sure it's what you ordered. Those mix-ups don't happen much nowadays, but I do remember a story about a friend of mine and a very expensive restaurant some years ago. His friend was showing off and ordered a bottle of a very expensive French wine from a certain year—an excellent vintage, you understand. The waiter duly took the order and returned to the table, bottle of wine in hand; but just as he was about to serve it the friend noticed that the waiter's finger was over the vintage on the label. When he was asked to move his finger it turned out that the bottle was from the right place but was of another, much cheaper vintage. My friend's friend was about to pay €200 for a €100 bottle of wine!

• Tasting the wine is the norm, to make sure it's okay. The waiter should offer, splashing a drop into your glass so you can taste it. When you're tasting wine, first give it a little sniff—does it smell winey or vinegary? If there's a vinegar note it could well be gone off; if it's musty it might be corked. If the wine is cloudy it may not have been stored properly, unless you've ordered some ancient vintage! However, if it's nice and clean and fresh it's yours, but make sure they come back to you to fill your glass properly!

• If you open a bottle and it's gone off, for whatever reason, the restaurant will replace it without question, as it gets a credit for spoiled bottles. There's absolutely no problem with that.

• I know that a lot of people don't really like waiters filling their glasses—they find it hard to keep track of what they're drinking—but there are generally sound reasons for their doing so. It could be a house policy to keep your glass topped up, as this means that more wine is being bought, certainly; but remember, it's also about service. I've seen people wrestling with a wine bucket on a stand and dripping water all over the place; refilling is the waiter's job. Also, it can be a bit of an embarrassment when you don't want to drink but the person opposite wants more—best to leave it in neutral hands, I think. You can always say to the waiter, 'Thanks very much, no wine for me.'

EATING AWKWARD FOOD

I'm always reminded of Leslie Nielsen, playing Frank Drebin, in *Naked Gun 2½* when I think of awkward food. Drebin's having dinner with President and Mrs Bush at the White House and pulls the leg off his lobster—whereupon it flies towards Mrs Bush's cleavage!

Lobster probably isn't the obstacle course it once was, when it was served whole at the table with a variety of implements. Nowadays, the lobster is generally halved for you, so it's easy to get the meat out. (Having said that, I have a friend I dread eating with, because she takes four hours to get through her lobster, eating every last bit of meat and digging around in the claws with the little fork provided for the purpose.) If you should be served a whole lobster you can attack it by first twisting off the claws to remove them from the body, then twisting the tail off in the same way. (Do this slowly if you want to avoid being Frank Drebin.) You'll be left with the body, then, and if you peel away the shell covering you'll get a nice big bit of meat; the green stuff at the end is the liver and is edible. You can dig around in the spiny legs for small pieces of meat—you'll get a fork for this—and then use your cracker, like a nutcracker, to crack the claws in order to get at the meat inside. Don't crack too hard or you'll end up with shell in your meat or by spraying your fellow-guests with lobster. It's all a bit of a palaver, but many people swear by fresh lobster with just a touch of butter. Make sure you have bowls of water, with slices of lemon in them, to wash your hands: eating lobster is a messy business. The same goes for eating crab, although, again, its shell and claws are generally served separately nowadays. A whole crab is very rich anyway.

I love **mussels**, even if they're a bit messy. When a steaming bowl of mussels arrives in front of you it should be accompanied by an empty bowl. This is where you put the shells once you've extracted the meat. You normally loosen the meat with the fork provided, or with the other side of the shell, which you use as a little scoop; dip it into the lovely white-wine sauce and eat it. Simple, if a little messy, as you'll have to hold onto the shell with one hand. You'll be supplied with finger bowls with lemony water in them to clean your hands at regular intervals.

The most important thing when eating **oysters** is that they should be fresh. They should look bright and shiny, smell of the sea and shrink slightly when you press them with your finger—yes, they're alive! They will be loosened from the shell for you and should arrive on a bed of crushed ice, with slices of lemon. Many people prefer to eat them just as they are, because the briny flavour is something they love; but if you find that a bit daunting, the French have a nice red-wine vinaigrette with tiny chopped shallots in it that they often drizzle on the oyster, and then it's straight down the hatch. Now, some people swear by chewing a few times before you swallow the oyster, just to get the flavour, but that depends on how adventurous you are!

Fish isn't as difficult to eat nowadays, because it's generally served in fillets, rather than whole; but if you're served a whole trout, for example, how do you eat it? To begin with, you can just lift the skin gently with your knife—unless you like fish skin—and push it off the flesh. Then, with your fork, hold the fish in place, so it doesn't slide off the plate, and push the flesh away from the spine gently. It should come away very easily. When you've finished one side of your fish, turn it over gently and tackle the other side in the same way.

When you're eating **lamb chops with the bone on or ribs**, pick them up and go at the meat with your teeth. Some books say not to, but I think it's quite acceptable as I can't honestly see how you can remove meat from ribs with a knife and fork. In any case, you're unlikely to be served ribs at a Michelin-starred restaurant. The same goes for chicken wings and drumsticks.

It's fine to eat small slices of **pizza** with your hands. Use the pizza-cutter first to cut slices—not huge flapping bits that will drip hot tomato sauce down your front! Some older people prefer to use a knife and fork, but I think pizza is a dish designed to be eaten with the hands.

Some people think **artichokes** are just too much trouble and prefer to buy the hearts in oil from the deli; but if you're served a whole artichoke, what you do is pluck the leaves off one by one and then scrape the meat off the fat end of the leaf with your teeth. You'll often get a sauce to dip them in. You then discard the rest of the leaf. When you get to the centre, the 'choke', you can cut it up into small pieces or eat it whole.

It may seem silly to list **bread** as an awkward food, but people are often confused about how to eat it in a restaurant. If you're served a roll, you don't hack at it with your knife, for the simple reason that you'll spray your fellow diners with breadcrumbs. You can either break off small bits of the roll and use the butter knife to butter it, before breaking another bit off, and so on, or you can gently prise it apart with your fingers and then butter each half. The trick is to use your fingers, as you can then control the spraying of crumbs. If you're served slices of home-made bread don't reach across and help yourself to whatever you fancy from the basket: ask your fellow diner to pass it to you and then select your slice, putting it on your plate and buttering it.

Spaghetti. To slurp or to bite, that is the question. I'm a biter myself: to slurp means to spatter spaghetti sauce all over my shirt. I twist the spaghetti around my fork, taking care not to put too much on it, then lift it to my mouth, hoping that the strands don't come loose. I don't use a spoon, although many people find it easier, and that's perfectly fine. Italians don't use a spoon to help them twirl their spaghetti; in fact, they find the whole idea very amusing. I don't cut it up into little bits either, although that's fine for children.

Once a rarity, *sushi* is commonplace nowadays. The correct way to eat a piece of sushi is to pincer it between your chopsticks, dip it in soy sauce and maybe a dab of wasabi—the very spicy paste that comes with Japanese food—and then bring it to your mouth. Apparently, if you're sharing a big plate of sushi you shouldn't use the bit of the chopstick that's been in your mouth to spear your next bit of sushi: instead, turn your chopsticks the other way around. If you're worried about dropping the sushi, it's just fine to bend a little closer to your plate—this is what Japanese people do. If you hate chopsticks it's actually better to pick the sushi up with your fingers, for practical reasons: if you try to jab it with a fork it'll fall apart.

The golden rule with *tacos, burritos and fajitas* is to eat sloppy versions with a knife and fork, and drier versions with your fingers. So, if you have a nice chicken fajita pick it up in your hand and eat it—yes, some chicken pieces will fall onto your plate, but it really is more practical than trying to cut into a flour tortilla with your knife and fork. The same goes for tacos, which are normally served with a 'dry' filling of minced meat and kidney beans. If it's terribly sloppy and saucy, by all means use a knife and fork.

DON'T FORGET YOUR TABLE MANNERS!

So, you've negotiated the wine list and ordered from the menu, and you're ready to tuck in. Before you do, though, remember your table manners. If we've been brought up well by our mothers and fathers we shouldn't need too many lessons in eating nicely, but there are a few guidelines that apply when we're eating out.

1. Your napkin should go on your knee, unless you're eating seafood, for which a bib will be provided.

2. Eat with your mouth closed, and don't talk with your mouth full.

3. If you have a terrible cold and need to blow your nose, try not to honk constantly into your tissue at the table. Wait until you can avoid it no longer and then nip out to the toilet. If you need to sneeze, turn away from the table and do so discreetly into your hanky—not into your napkin. That way you don't spread your germs all over the place.

4. No elbows on the table or waving your cutlery around. The same goes for dropping your food onto your lap. Some of us get a bit distracted, but take it slowly and you'll be fine.

5. Of course, no belching! You've appreciated the lovely food, but a demonstration of how much isn't necessary.

6. Whether to slurp or not depends on where you're eating: you wouldn't slurp soup at a Michelin-starred restaurant; instead, you'd scoop it up gently into the spoon in the way described on the website www.etiquettescholar.com: 'Hold the soup spoon by resting the end of the handle on your middle finger, with your thumb on top. Dip the spoon sideways into the soup at the near edge of the bowl, then skim from the front of the bowl to the back. Sip from the side of the spoon, avoid improper table manners and do not to slurp. To retrieve the last spoonful of soup, slightly tip the bowl away from you and spoon in the way that works best.' Now you know!

But if you're eating, say, Japanese noodles, it's considered perfectly acceptable to slurp. In fact, according to the Japanese noodle restaurant Wagamama, 'above all, you must slurp the soup as noisily as possible... The slurping oxygenates the soup and cools it so as not to scald the roof of the mouth,' because ramen noodles are served piping hot.

8. If you need to remove a fish bone from your mouth you can use your fingers. The same goes for olive stones and peach stones. If you've encountered a nasty piece of gristle, don't yank it out of your mouth: push it out onto your fork and discreetly place it on the plate.

9. Don't reach across other people to get at the butter: ask them to pass it to you.

10. If your fellow diners haven't finished yet, don't get up and wander off: wait until it's polite to do so and then excuse yourself from the table.

The head of cabbage

Talking about food reminds me of the story of the head of cabbage, which also involves complaining—see below!

A young fellow worked in Superquinn some years ago. It had a very upmarket clientele, being at the posher end of the supermarket market. The young man came into work on a Monday morning, having been out all night on the booze, and his head was absolutely bursting—a terrible hangover. He was working in the fruit and veg section, taking in a huge order, it being a Monday morning, and he was praying, 'Please don't let anybody talk to me, because I'm just going to die.'

And then he heard a voice behind him. 'Excuse me.'

Please don't let that be for me, he thought. He turned round, to see a very well-dressed elderly woman, holding a head of Dutch cabbage—the tight, football-shaped one—in her hand.

He sighed wearily. 'Yes, madam, can I help you?'

'Could I have half a head of cabbage?' she asked, in a very classy accent.

This young fellow had never seen or heard of half a head of cabbage, so he said, 'I'm sorry?'

She repeated, 'Could I have half a head of cabbage?'

'We don't do half heads of cabbage,' he replied, half wondering if 'Candid Camera' was around the corner.

At this, she looked very cross. 'I beg your pardon. I shop in Superquinn in Blanchardstown, and they always give me half a head of cabbage, because I live on my own. Please check with your supervisor.'

He thought, For God's sake, and shuffled off through the plastic doors into the storeroom. 'Joe?' he called. 'Are you in there?'

His supervisor stepped out from behind a row of twenty cases of oranges and said, 'What's up?'

'There's a wan out here, and my head's feckin' killin' me, and do you know what she wants? She wants half a head of cabbage,' the young fellow moaned.

'What?'

'What am I going to tell her? She's looking for an effin' half head of cabbage, and my head's ready to burst, and, you know, she's going on and on...'

As the young man spoke, Joe began to wave his arms frantically, but to no avail, because the fellow continued to give out. 'Effin' oul' one outside...'

And then the penny dropped. The young man turned round, to find the woman standing beside him. She'd followed him inside and had clearly heard all the effin' and blindin'. He turned to her and smiled brightly. 'Oh, and you see this lovely lady here? She's going to take the other half, Joe.'

Quick thinking...

HAVE YOU ENJOYED YOUR MEAL?

Unlike our lovely lady in Superquinn, the Irish people are terrible at complaining. They say nothing at all at the time and then go home and complain afterwards. And, thanks to TripAdvisor and other websites, increasingly they have somewhere to vent. I'll be looking at 'venting' in the next chapter; but, let me tell you, there's not a hotelier in the world who has escaped a bad review on TripAdvisor. It goes with the territory nowadays.

I looked at complaining in Chapter 3, so you'll remember that I feel it's better to complain quickly and quietly when you're in a restaurant, particularly about food items, because you're likely to have your complaint remedied quickly. At the Park we have a system whereby returned items from the restaurant go to the top of the queue, because that person is at a table with others, eating their main course, and doesn't want to have to wait half an hour. Steaks and salads are the usual returned items—steaks because they haven't been cooked the way the customer likes them, and salads because the customer doesn't like the dressing.

If the complaint goes beyond a returned item the head waiter should come over and apologise immediately, even if the complaint doesn't seem reasonable, because it's hard to define what a 'reasonable' complaint is. And you do get professional complainers.

If you do need to complain about food in a restaurant, please see the tips on complaining in Chapter 3 (p. 66). If your complaint is serious and involves bad hygiene, the Food Safety Authority of Ireland (www.fsai.ie) will be able to advise you.

PAYING THE BILL

You'll often find that, having hovered over the table all night, your waiter disappears at the crucial moment: when you need to pay the bill. This is because they've gone to serve other customers, leaving you to linger over dessert. If time is an issue, mention it to them as you order dessert: 'I'll also have the bill in a few moments, please,' as it can take time to put together.

When the bill arrives, check it discreetly to make sure everything has been included, and nothing added. If you'll be sharing the bill decide beforehand to split it between everyone equally——no totting up of desserts and petits fours at the table in order to see if Mary should be paying five euro more than John! Normally, if you've just joined the party for dessert, you won't have to shell out for the whole meal, but otherwise I'm afraid it's fair game: you may have eaten only a salad, while Jim had a steak, but good manners dictate that you pay up.

Then nominate one person to pay the bill, to gather together the money or cards and to negotiate with the waiter, who doesn't need a table of competing voices, as well as a raft of debit cards! If you're in a posh restaurant you'll be given a wallet with the bill in it. Put your cash or cards inside and place it conveniently on the table for your water; leave some money sticking out so they can can see that you've paid. Check if service is included in the bill. If not, you'll need to devise a tip, generally 15 per cent. Even if service is included, many waiters appreciate a bit of cash. You can leave this when the bill has been settled——on the table is fine.

And you're done, hopefully having had a wonderful evening, having had the confidence to order your food and wine with aplomb and having relaxed and enjoyed the company.

Social
media

'A lot of people say that social media is making us all dumber,
but I not think that.'
—Unknown

EVEN THOUGH I'm a bit old-fashioned in other departments, I'm quite a keen user of technology, believe it or not. I have my smartphone and all my apps, and even though I'm not a Twitter or Facebook user I'm happy to use Viber and Skype and that kind of thing. However, with all the various social media services about, and with new ones coming on stream practically every day, many people are unsure about how to use them and, more importantly, about how to exercise good manners online.

To me it's quite simple: behave online as you'd behave in your daily life, with courtesy and respect for other people. If you remember this core rule you'll be just fine. That is not to say that there aren't some simple guidelines to follow!

E-MAILING ESSENTIALS

While not all of us use Twitter and Snapchat, we'll nearly all have used e-mail at one stage or another, and we'd probably agree that it isn't quite as formal as the letter, but neither is it like chatting to your best friend. There are rules for sending e-mails, even if they haven't been spelled out.

- I always use the greeting 'Dear X' when I'm writing an e-mail to someone I don't know. 'Hi' or 'Mary Kate' or 'Hello there' are all too informal. However, you don't need to use the awful form 'Dear Francis Brennan', which I just hate. 'Dear Francis' is just fine: the formality is conveyed by the use of 'Dear'. The same goes for your sign-off. Remember when we were at school and learned the formula 'Dear Sir... Yours faithfully' or 'Dear Francis... Yours sincerely'? I don't think there's any real need for that kind of formality in an e-mail. However, 'See ya' isn't right either. I like 'Sincerely, Francis' if I don't know the person, or 'Best regards' or 'All the best'.

- DON'T WRITE YOUR E-MAILS IN CAPITAL LETTERS: IT SOUNDS LIKE YOU'RE YELLING! See what I mean?

- Use correct punctuation and spelling, and don't abbreviate. E-mailing is not like texting: 'cul8r' is not acceptable in an e-mail. Before you send your e-mail, check the spelling and punctuation. If in doubt, make sure your spelling check is switched on, so that it will indicate any misspellings.

- If someone has sent you an e-mail, acknowledge it, even if you haven't got time to respond just yet. The same goes for when you're away: set a standard message to let them know you'll be in touch. However, I would be a little careful here: 'always on' culture does mean that answering e-mails at unsocial times is creeping in. Think carefully before you reply. Do you really want to get into an exchange of e-mails at the weekend or at one o'clock in the morning?

- Learn the difference between your 'reply to sender' and 'reply to all' buttons. Many people have found this out to their cost when they've received an e-mail and accidentally replied to the entire office, particularly if their message contained negative comments about a colleague or client.

- While we're on the subject of 'negative' comments, just don't make them in e-mails. If you say something silly about a friend in person, or put your foot in it, you can just apologise. But if you commit it to e-mail it can't be taken back. Just as you'd scan a letter before sending it, or lift your pen before writing something unpleasant about Auntie Mary, don't be tempted to let rip in an e-mail. It can be a very public form of communication.

- You might have a great collection of jokes or photos of dogs you'd like to share, but only do so with people you know are happy to look at them. Some people find that a joke really cheers them up; others think they get in the way of their working day.

- Try not to use e-mail for really important events that require a personal touch. E-mail may be the most convenient choice, but picking up the phone shows that you're making an effort to have a real conversation. I also prefer to use the phone if I want to share important news or invite people to dinner or any big occasion—it's just more personal.

TEXTING

I think texting should really be used only for essential messages: making arrangements, scheduling meetings—that kind of thing. I know that the youngsters of Ireland won't agree with me here, but I'm firm about this. It's certainly very useful, but it's an impersonal way of communicating, and I like to remember that.

I have a friend who always texts me, 'How are you, Francis?' when he hasn't seen me for a bit. I have no clue how to reply in ten words! And imagine if I had some upsetting news to share... To me, that's not a proper chat: it's just an exchange of information. The same goes for breaking dates or for anything that requires the making of an excuse: 'Sorry, can't make ur wedding,' is not right, I have to say. And as for breaking up by text message… need I say more!

'Text-speak' is another hotly debated topic. Now that we have predictive text there's really no need to use abbreviations, unless you're a teenager, in which case it's absolutely part of the lingo. For the rest of us, we just look a bit silly LOL'ing and OMG'ing all over the place. The same goes for smiley faces—lovely for youngsters, but not for grown-ups.

If you receive a text message when out and about, resist the temptation to break off your conversation, or screech to a halt in the car, to see who's sent it. There's something about social media that makes us think we have to jump up and respond immediately; but remember, you're in charge. Wait until it's convenient for you to reply. If you think it's urgent, excuse yourself first and then look at the message.

PRIVACY

I like my privacy and rarely give out my mobile phone number, not to mention posting photos of myself on Facebook, but social media have led to a breakdown in boundaries about privacy. It mystifies me why you'd want to upload photos of yourself drunk or eating a massive hamburger, but that's just me! To me it goes without saying that if you wouldn't be happy passing a photo of your ingrown toenail across the garden fence to your neighbour, why would you be happy posting any kind of compromising picture on a social network where millions upon millions of people could get to see and share it?

Privacy also extends to your friends and family. We all love taking photos at weddings and parties, particularly now that it's so easy with our smartphones, and then we like to post them on Facebook or Instagram so that we can show our friends what we've been doing. It's all so instant, which brings its own problems.

Remember the slide shows and video presentations of years ago? Uncle Brian would take photos at a wedding with his special slide film, and, weeks later, family and friends would gather round for tea and biscuits in a darkened living room while the slide carousel rattled through a couple of dozen slides. Everyone aahed and giggled together, cringing when the camera caught them at just the wrong moment. But they knew that the slides were for their consumption only: after the show Uncle Brian would return the pictures to their box, where they'd gather dust quite happily. If there was anything that shouldn't be seen, the only people who would see it would be Uncle Brian and maybe the chemist developing the photos or slides.

Today, of course, it's different, and photographs pop up on social media almost the moment they're taken. And that's the problem. Because the images are instant, people don't think before posting them. If you post a picture of a friend misbehaving, you might think it's hilarious, but what about your friend, who doesn't want their mother to see the photo of them the worse for wear? It's not just your privacy but theirs that's at stake. I think it's best to ask people's permission before posting pictures of them online. Show them the photo on your camera or phone and mention that you want to post it online. People will often be happy for you to, but sometimes they won't be, so respect that.

The other thing to note about privacy is that you should regularly check your privacy settings on Twitter and Facebook to make sure that what you want to be private is in fact private. Also, make sure you adapt your settings for the various people in your life: have different groups with whom you share different things. Don't let your boss see the picture of you swigging from a huge tankard of beer, when you meant it for your sister!

About your 'friends' on social media—Facebook friends are not the same as real ones, so be careful about what you post and who you let see it. As for 'friending', don't friend your teenage kids: it's just a bit creepy, and it won't make you look cool. A survey by two academics in Australia on the use of Facebook found that lonely people were far more likely to share personal information than others, therefore leaving themselves open to exploitation. It's obviously distressing, because Facebook isn't the real world, and it's important to remember that.

COMMENTS

'Tact is the art of making a point without making an enemy.'—Isaac Newton

Nowhere is the instantaneousness of social media more obvious than in the comments sections of social media. It's a minefield, as many people have found out to their cost. In days gone by, if something upset us or made us angry, the only people who would know would be our friends, or maybe Joe Duffy! Now all we have to do is jump on to Facebook or Twitter to vent our spleen. And then we have all the time in the world to regret our little broadside about the post arriving late, the phone call that was never made or that perceived personal slight. The problem is that it's then too late: it's there for all to see and to share. And remember, retweeting offensive or inaccurate tweets can often land you in very hot water, as some have discovered.

As far as I'm concerned, it's back to those basic rules of good manners: don't post anything online that you wouldn't be happy saying face to face. And remember, all the other users on the internet are not virtual—they're real—and it pays to treat them as people. Here are some other useful rules when it comes to posting comments:

- No insults or negative language in response to something someone else has said. ('I can't believe you could be so stupid…'—that kind of thing.) If you wouldn't say it to the person face to face, don't put it up for all the world to see, and don't hide behind your username or handle. Some people can begin to believe in the identity they've created for themselves online and can then behave in a way in which they would never dream of behaving in real life. Such people also believe, wrongly, that their nasty comments give them some status in the virtual world. Who was it who said, 'If you can't say something nice, don't say nothing at all'?

- Trolling is an unpleasant part of life for so many internet users. Genuine people post videos of a school play, for example, only to find that it receives unpleasant and some-times even nasty comments. If you have been the victim of trolling, see if you can alter your settings to cut out comments, and always report it to the moderator. For serious cases of bullying or harassment the Gardaí have some very useful help on their website, www.garda.ie. Among their suggestions are:

1. Don't reply to any messages that harass you—the sender is trying to engage you, but this won't work if you don't reply.
2. Keep a record of all unsavoury messages, as they may be needed in an investigation.
3. Block the sender.
4. If the harassment is serious or could be criminal, report it to the Gardaí.

- Everyone has an opinion, even if you disagree with it, so respect that. If you want to disagree, do so politely and then express your own opinion, without resorting to personal language.

- Because people from all over the world use English-language comments pages, grammar and spelling will not always be as a native speaker would have them. So be tactful if correcting other people's English, and if you're a native speaker always use proper grammar and spelling yourself. Also, if moderating, don't tinker with anyone else's posts without mentioning it.

- If you notice that a friend or acquaintance has overstepped the mark on social media, you might politely point out the error of their ways and offer them a chance to put things right before anyone else but the two of you notice.

- 'Please' and 'thank you' are as welcome in social media as they are in real life. If someone says something nice about you on social media, you can say thank you by sending them a private message or e-mail.

TAKING PHOTOS

With smartphones having such brilliant cameras, taking photos has almost become a reflex for so many of us. Often we don't stop to actually look at whatever it is we're snapping: we just click and commit it to our phone's memory. And with the arrival of the 'selfie', Heaven help us... nowhere is safe! I had to laugh when I heard an election official reminding voters that it's against the law to take selfies in the polling booth in the local and European elections. Why on earth you'd want to do that is beyond me!

I think it's important to think before you click, particularly at formal occasions. It's very common now for the bride and groom's walk down the aisle to be accompanied by the flashing of mobile phones, which seems to spoil the magic of the moment, as far as I'm concerned. What's wrong with just looking at the lovely scene?

I've talked about privacy above, but other people's wedding photos are not for public consumption, I would think, and I wouldn't post them online—certainly not without getting permission. And when it comes to 'tagging' photographs (that is, naming somebody in a photo that's posted online, as my technological friends tell me), do so with extreme caution. That person may not want their name to appear all over the place.

It's also important, when you whip your mobile out to photograph something, to ask yourself if it's appropriate. People photograph just about everything, including car accidents and other incidents, some of which involve criminal action. Again, think before you point. Could you be helping instead of filming? Should you be calling the police instead of recording the incident? And if it's something fun, like a family party or a concert, why not try experiencing it instead of just taking a photo of it?

COMPLAINING ONLINE

We all know how hard it can be to complain or to get redress for online purchases. I know that, if you have a complaint, you have the same rights under EU regulations as someone who has bought something over the counter, but that's little comfort when you want to make a complaint or get a refund but can't find a single human being to talk to.

I learned this to my cost when I made a hotel booking by means of a certain payment processor, which turned into a bit of a nightmare. I booked a hotel in London but then needed to cancel ten days later—all perfectly fine within the terms of my booking. But when I came to ask for a refund, things got sticky. The payment processor said it was the hotel's problem, and the hotel said it was the payment processor's! It took me five months and a file the size of a telephone book to get my refund. And at no stage did I speak to an actual person; instead, I communicated by e-mail with a succession of different names. It was all very impersonal and inefficient.

Some years ago, at the dawn of the internet age, I was on the board of the Small Luxury Hotels of the World. This organisation grouped together hotels in the luxury bracket so that bookings could be made online throughout the group, with a commission going to the SLHW. We were having a lot of difficulty with our accounts department because of staff turnover and also because people would book online but then cancel with the hotel itself, leaving the organisation waiting for a commission that wouldn't be forthcoming. At one particular meeting a man called Vikram Oberoi was at the table. He was a member of the Oberoi family, which operates a number of luxury hotels in India and the Middle East. 'It's simple,' he said, in response to our accounting headache. 'Just take your accounts department to India.'

We had no idea what he was talking about, but, of course, he was very far-sighted. He could see the benefits of having a local, stable call-centre work force, as well as the fact that continuity would really work to solve our problem. And he was right! It looks as if some large corporations, such as banks, are beginning to understand this now, after all this time: people want to speak to an actual human being when they have a problem, and to be able to talk to just that one person, not every member of the complaints department. Many of them now employ 'relationship managers', who you can contact so that you don't get bounced around every department in the company.

All of this is just brilliant, but remember: you're not covered by the same consumer rights when you buy from an auction site or from a private individual, of which there are many online. That's not to say that you shouldn't buy from them, just that you should be aware that you won't have any redress if there are problems. Look carefully at the seller's 'history', that is, the positive and negative reviews they've had from past buyers, and use a payment-processing service that offers protection for online purchases. But check their terms and conditions carefully, as it's not a 'blanket' protection.

I hope I won't have frightened you off using social media in this chapter. I can see that they offer so many brilliant opportunities—there's so much fun to be had with them, and so much to learn—but when you're communicating with the whole world, of course, you need to exercise caution and to remember that you're talking to other human beings. In life and online, it pays to remember Matthew 7:12. 'So in everything, do to others what you would have them do to you.'

Epilogue:

IT'S THE LITTLE THINGS

BEFORE I came to write this postscript, I read again through my introduction, where I talked about the three Cs—caring, consideration and community—and how important they are to me. I hope that, reading this book, you will understand what I mean by these and also that you have a bit of fun in the process.

I didn't set out to lecture anybody on the 'right' way to behave. In fact, as I wrote, I kept having to ask myself if I was quite as mannerly as I'd thought! Writing a book on manners and etiquette can sometimes give you a lot to live up to.

Having written at length about home and family, restaurants, mobile phones, eating out and looking nice, I came to realise that, essentially, there are only a few core ideas that I try to carry with me every day.

1.

SMILE.

2.

HOLD THE DOOR OPEN FOR OTHERS.

3.

ASK HOW SOMEONE IS—
AND LISTEN TO THEIR RESPONSE.

4.

BE POSITIVE.

5.

DON'T FORGET YOURSELF.

If you remember these five things every day, you'll be just fine. You'll also find that you get more out of life if you put more in. I'm not normally a fan of motivational speakers, but I like this saying of Brian Tracy's: 'Successful people are always looking for opportunities to help others. Unsuccessful people are always asking, "What's in it for me?"' Helping others is not a sign of weakness: it's a strength.

I know it might seem silly to think that just five little things can make a difference, but, believe me, they do, and I've always felt that it's best to set yourself little goals that are achievable. You're not going to change who you are overnight, but you can make small, positive changes in order to make your life happier. Taking on too much is like telling yourself that you're going to run the London Marathon, having never even donned a pair of running shoes—and then facing the inevitable disappointment when you don't make it. Far better, I think, to aim to run around the block first and to feel delighted with yourself when you achieve that goal. You can then build on that run—and, who knows, in a year you might well run that marathon. Rome wasn't built in a day. The same applies to good manners, and indeed to making any kind of change in life.

1. SMILING

Nowadays it can be tempting to go around with a preoccupied look on our faces, because we have so much to think about and so much to remember in our busy lives; but whose life hasn't been improved by a smile? By that I don't mean a 'Cheer up, love, it might never happen' kind of smile, which is frankly maddening, or that we should ourselves smile when things are very difficult or we're having serious life problems—no, I mean the kind of smile that cheers other people up, that makes them think life isn't so bad after all. Smiles are the currency of our daily lives.

As with everything these days, there's a 'smile' survey: a group of researchers at Bangor University attempted to put a monetary value on smiling. It's a third of a penny, apparently; but if you exchange a number of smiles with somebody in a conversation it really adds up. And, more importantly, those who were studied in the survey were far more receptive to a 'genuine' smile, which reaches the eyes, than to a 'polite' one. So, practise your smile today and start using it! And when you're out and about in your local area, smile and say hello to people. Maybe one or two will think you're a bit mad, but most people will smile right back and go about their day with a smile on their face too.

2. OPENING THE DOOR FOR OTHERS

It might seem odd to consider holding the door open a core principle in manners, but think about it: How many times a day do you go in and out of doors in public buildings, shopping centres, churches, doctors' surgeries? Imagine if you just let the door swing closed behind you every time. You'd have a lot of annoyed people on the other side! Now imagine what it would be like if, instead, you just turned round to check if there was somebody behind you and then held the door open for them. Yes, you might expend a millisecond of time, but they'll feel just great, and so will you. It's a little thing, but, as I've come to realise in writing this book, it's the little things that really count. And I firmly believe that holding doors open is not just the job of the chivalrous man: it's the job of the chivalrous woman too.

3. 'HOW ARE YOU?'

Every day we ask people how they are. It's an Irish thing, isn't it? 'How are you, Mary?' 'How are you, John?' And do we ever listen to the reply? I'm as guilty as everyone else here, and I have to remind myself every day that if I ask someone how they are, I need to listen to what they say, just the same as if somebody asks me, 'How are you, Francis?' I'd just love them to listen to an account of my journey into the studio or of the difficult customer I checked out that morning. It really matters: it means that someone else has acknowledged my life and that I've acknowledged theirs.

4. THE POWER OF POSITIVE THINKING

Endless books have been written about the powers of positive thinking and the benefits of thinking about your life only in positive terms. But actually there's a whole school of thought now that suggests that being positive all the time could actually be bad for us: it might make us afraid to face the realities of our lives. The psychologists Julie Norem and Nancy Cantor did a series of tests on people who they described as 'defensive pessimists', that is, people who foresaw the worst outcome of a job interview, for example. They compared them with 'strategic optimists' and found that both groups actually achieved the same results in the interviews. The so-called defensive pessimists used their worst-case scenarios to control anxiety by working hard to prepare for, and nail, that interview, instead of assuming that they'd sail through—a clever strategy, when you think about it, and one that might actually help people cope with lives that often don't work out as planned. Obviously, this is a very simplified version of their argument, but it's all in Norem's book *The Positive Power of Negative Thinking* (2001), if you're interested!

For me, the key is to be essentially optimistic about life: be honest with yourself about any difficulties you might be facing, but be hopeful that things will work out in time. I suppose I might call it 'positive realism'! By this I mean trying not to succumb to anxiety and negativity and focusing instead on the rich benefits of family and life.

5. DON'T FORGET YOURSELF...

Self-love and self-care don't mean self-absorption and self-obsession, as you'll see below in my ten tips for adding sparkle to life. If we don't look after ourselves we won't be able to give our best to others. So, finish that book you've been meaning to read, go on that walk, make that call to the friend who you know will cheer you up, wear that dress you bought for Jane's wedding—so what if it's for 'good wear' only: life's too short!

ESSENTIAL EXTRAS FOR LIFE

Try to remember those five little things above. I really hope they'll make your day happier. But what if you want to add a little sparkle to life—to make things just that little bit more special for yourself and those around you? When I first thought about it I wrote a list of nice things—lovely table settings, nice fresh flowers, clean towels in the bathroom—and I was all set to write about them. But then I paused for a moment: these can certainly make life brighter, but I think the question goes a bit deeper than that. All the fresh towels in the world won't work if you don't enjoy life. And enjoying life is what it's all about.

I think that, first of all, you have to be 'real'. We spend a lot of time looking at celebrities these days, and admiring them, and sometimes even wanting to be them. But that's not real: it's a fantasy world. What's real is the world around us: the outdoors, our friends and family, fun and laughter, maybe our pets, our hobbies. And manners and etiquette put a shine on all that. It's elegance, really. And elegance isn't a snooty word; it isn't about putting on airs: it's about being yourself. We can't all be the life and soul of the party. We can't all host a party for forty people and make it look easy, or tell jokes that make the whole room erupt with laughter. But we can be our best selves, every day.

Here are ten things I try to do every day to make life that bit more special... for myself and for others around me. See if they work for you.

1.

GET OUT INTO THE FRESH AIR

I freely admit that I spend much of my time in my car. I live in the countryside in Co. Kerry and wouldn't get anywhere at all if I didn't drive. I have to drive all over the country when I'm filming 'At Your Service', and when I'm not driving I'm flying. I'm afraid that my carbon footprint is fairly high! But one thing that works just a treat for my well-being, I've found, is spending time in the open air every day. Just a short walk, or pulling a few weeds in the garden, really helps me feel calmer and happier.

You don't have to have a huge garden to do this, or live in the countryside: you can grow a few herbs or lettuces in pots on your balcony if you have no outdoor space. There are lots of ideas for 'city' gardeners these days, from allotments to open spaces that have been planted by a group of local gardeners and that make urban areas look brighter.

Getting back to nature is even more important, I'd imagine, if you're a parent. So many parents drive their children to scheduled activities nowadays that young people haven't got the connection to the outdoors that we had when growing up. Prof. Richard Louv has written a number of books on the topic, and he calls it 'nature deficit disorder', which I think describes it perfectly. I'm not a parent, but I understand the great benefits that being outdoors as a child had for me: it helped to make me more resourceful and independent, as well as more used to working out danger and risk for myself. And now some parents are beginning to realise the benefits of outdoor play and are organising play sessions on their streets, with a parent keeping a general eye on things, largely because traffic is much more an issue now than it was in my day. What a brilliant idea.

2.

SPEND TIME WITH LOVED ONES

At the end of the day, family is all we've got, whether it's our blood family or a group of close friends we might have built around us. All the rest is just decoration, as far as I'm concerned. When we shuffle off this mortal coil we won't be able to take the Volvo with us, or the prized collection of china, so it really pays to nurture our relationships with others. I don't wish for a moment to trivialise serious family issues or problems; I'd just like to talk in general about the benefits of close relationships. Here are a few ideas:

- Spend fifteen minutes a day with your teenage son or daughter, focusing just on them and asking them how their day went; or spend fifteen minutes playing with your toddler. Giving them your undivided attention will really give them a boost.

- Drop in to see Auntie Mary for a quick cup of tea the next time you're passing. Don't tell yourself that you're in a hurry to get to the gym and that you'll do it next week, because we have no idea what the next week will bring. In Ireland we've lost the habit of 'just dropping by'— understandably, perhaps, with so many people out at work. Maybe it's one we should pick up again.

- Ring your friends for a chat before they ring you. I don't know about you, but I have a list of people in my head to phone, and I keep thinking, I really must call... But then they call you, and you're delighted, but you feel a bit guilty. Put a reminder on your phone to call them first. They'll be thrilled.

- If you won't have time to see a friend for a while, find a funny postcard or quotation you know they'll like and drop them a line. Or text them (I know...) to say that you're thinking of them and will be in touch as soon as you can.

- I have a friend who always turns up with a little gift at dinner parties—not a bottle of wine or a box of chocolates but a book she thinks I'll find interesting, or a plant that will look good in the kitchen window. I really appreciate the thought she puts into these gifts, and I know how much she values our friendship. Try doing this for a friend sometime. I find that it really works to stockpile little gifts I find on my travels that I know my friends will like.

- If you have a little difficulty or misunderstanding with a friend, try to resolve it quickly. Don't let it fester.

3.

SAY THANK YOU

Every day, thank people—whether it's the person who hands you your morning latte on the way to the Luas stop, your child's teacher, the lollipop lady or the man in the garage who tots up the price of your fuel—it's about treating others with courtesy, but it's also about recognising that we're all human and like to feel good and to feel appreciated. Some people think it's hilarious that Irish people always thank the bus driver, for example, when they get off the bus, but I think it's a lovely thing to do—a sign that we haven't forgotten our manners.

4.

BE 'MINDFUL'—AND LIVE IN THE MOMENT

I used to think that mindfulness was maybe a bit of a new gimmick, but so many people now practise mindfulness and find it such a help that I've been proved wrong. Beaumont Hospital in Dublin even has a Mindfulness and Relaxation Centre to help combat illness and stress. Mindfulness is hard to describe precisely, but it involves concentrating on your breathing and your body for short periods of time, and maybe also repeating a short phrase or 'mantra'. It's a form of meditation, if you like, but a very simple and straightforward one that will really become part of your life. It's all about learning to live in the 'now' and not worrying about the past or the future. The Beaumont Hospital website has some very useful free exercises on mindfulness, relaxation and worry management, with audio files that you can download. You'll find these at www.beaumont.ie/marc.

5.

LOOK AFTER YOURSELF

No, this doesn't mean being selfish or putting yourself before others—quite the opposite. There's a big difference between being kind to yourself and thinking only about your own needs. I think that many of us, particularly parents and carers, can forget ourselves because we are so used to putting other people first and to catering for their needs. I always say, try to do one nice thing for yourself every day. That doesn't really mean eating chocolate biscuits, although that's okay too! It means taking half an hour to watch your favourite programme or spending fifteen minutes blow-drying your hair, or going for a walk, or talking to a friend who you know will make you laugh—anything that makes you feel good. I realise that, as life goes on, it isn't made up of the big things—the 'important' moments—but lots of little moments like these, and they all count.

6.

SHARE A JOKE AND A LAUGH

When we are children it seems that we can truly laugh, from giggles to belly laughs, but as we get older we lose the knack for it, and that's a pity, I think. Of course, being a grown-up means that we have our responsibilities and our worries, but a laugh will really help to put them in perspective. You're not making light of your problems, just seeing that there are other things in life too. There's nothing I like better than a silly joke, whether it's a knock-knock joke shared with one of my nieces or nephews, or a funny anecdote. I love funny stories, as you've probably gathered! I like telling them, and I like listening to them. Other people like looking at YouTube videos of funny cats or parrots that can sing Abba songs—and why not? Anything that helps lighten the load. And health professionals are now beginning to realise the benefits of humour and laughter for mental health. One Canadian man, David Granirer, has turned to stand-up comedy in order to help him cope with depression and is now leading comedy workshops for people with mental-health issues.

7.

COMPLIMENT SOMEONE ON THEIR APPEARANCE OR EFFORT

This has the real feel-good factor, as far as I'm concerned. If I admire a man's tie or a woman's hair I just say it. 'I love your hair' or 'Your shoes are wonderful' or 'This cake is delicious.' Or, to a child, 'I think you made such a big effort with your homework.' If someone tells me they like my tie or my new shoes it really makes me walk with a spring in my step.

And the other side of that is, if someone compliments you, to say thank you. Otherwise you'll 'take the good out of it,' as my mother used to say. Don't deflect the compliment by saying, 'Sure it only cost me a fiver in Penney's!' We all know the joke about the visitor to Ireland who thought Penney's meant 'thank you', because when one person said, 'Love your skirt,' the other would reply, 'Penney's!'

8.

DO ONE THING FOR SOMEBODY ELSE EVERY DAY

Remember the 'good deed for the day'? It isn't some kind of relic from the era when Ireland was 100 per cent Catholic. Doing something nice for someone every day isn't just a Christian duty: it's a psychological boost for them and for you. The next time you see your elderly neighbour struggling with their wheelie bin, offer to take it out for them. When you see a mother struggling to get a buggy onto the bus, help her carry it on. Give up your seat on the train for a person who needs it. Of course, it's easier just to do nothing and to go on about your day, but you'll be surprised how much better you'll feel when you've done something nice for someone else.

9.

COMMUNICATE

Write letters or phone people and chat. I know, it's hard nowadays. The irony is that now that we're all 'connected' twenty-four hours a day, we probably communicate less than ever. We're so used to exchanging short, informational text messages or business e-mails that we have forgotten the art of chatting on the phone or writing somebody a short letter or postcard. As in everything else in life, try to make things achievable. Don't tell yourself you'll devote two hours to writing a letter to your old friend in Australia: try half an hour to jot down a 'How are you?' postcard or to send them something that lets them know you're thinking of them. And when you feel the urge to whip out your mobile phone and hammer out a quick text to a friend you haven't seen in a while, pause for a second. Wouldn't it be nicer if you phoned? If you haven't got half an hour to chat, just say so: 'I thought I'd give you a quick ring before I put the dinner on'—that kind of thing.

10.

BE PATIENT

We all know the sayings 'Patience is a virtue' and 'Good things come to those who wait,' but we've got out of the patience habit, I think. It's hard these days, and I count myself among those who I wish would be a bit more patient. Life now moves so quickly that it's hard to resist the urge to tut with impatience in a queue or if the bus is ten minutes late. And then we huff and puff when a less able-bodied person shuffles on ahead of us very slowly, or we roll our eyes to heaven as someone fumbles with their change at the supermarket. And we Irish people know how impatient we can be as drivers, tooting our horns all over the place and yelling out our car windows. The instantaneousness of everything has made us impatient.

But the problem is also that we can be impatient with ourselves, expecting our lives to become fabulous overnight or imagining that we will achieve our goals instantly. I've tried to think of a few ways in which we might slow down.

- Take a deep breath and count to ten. It may seem obvious, but if we do it often enough it becomes a habit.

- Try to enjoy the process of something you're doing at that moment—that book you're writing or that run around the park in preparation for a marathon—rather than thinking of it only as a means to an end. As the journalist Sydney J. Harris said, 'Happiness is a journey, not a place.'

- Friends of mine who are parents say it's great to give yourself, instead of your child, a 'time out'. If you're a parent, and your patience is wearing thin, try popping into the bedroom for five minutes' deep breathing, or bashing the pillow—whatever works!

- If waiting for a bus or queuing at an ATM makes you fume, try to do something else while you're waiting: whip out a book or your smartphone. Or, even better, practise your mindfulness exercises. Distraction can really help to diffuse impatience.

- If helping your child with their homework drives you up the wall, have you thought of asking your spouse or an older child to help? Know your triggers and avoid them.

✳

I really hope you've enjoyed reading this book as much as I've enjoyed writing it. I did indeed enjoy the journey: it really helped me to remember what's important to me, and I've enjoyed sharing it with all of you. Be mindful, be kind and be happy!

THE END